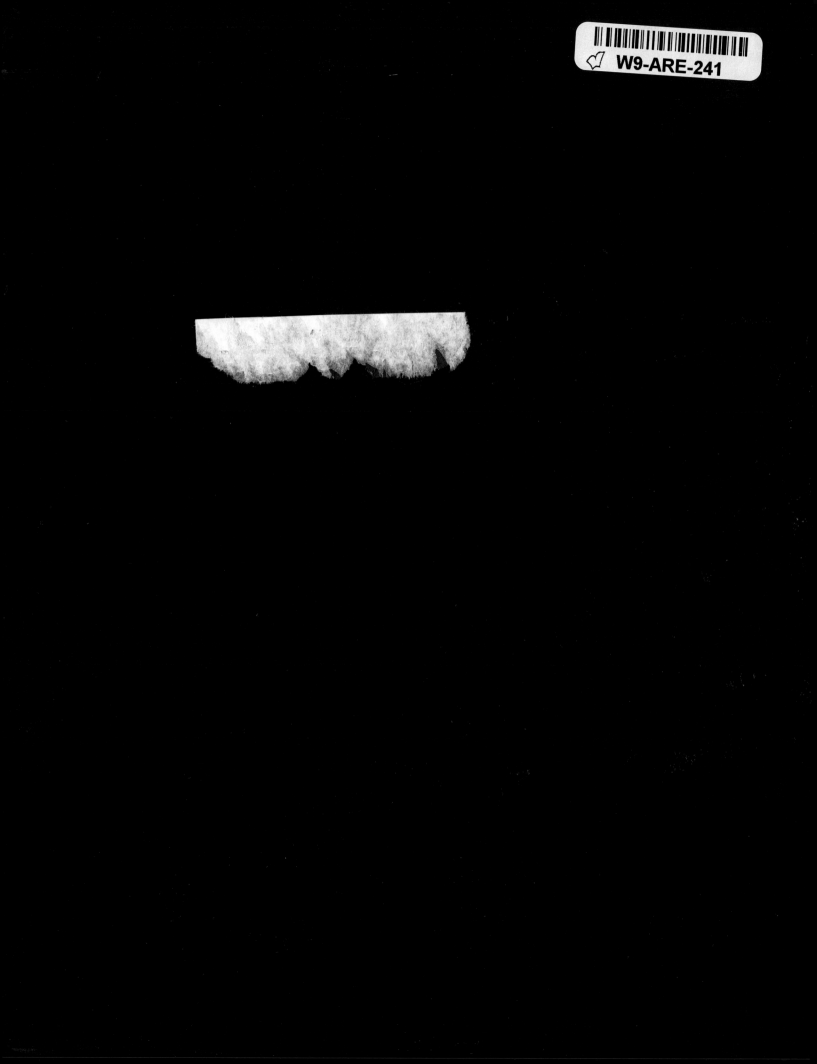

Underground fighters, armed with weapons air-dropped by the Allies, take cover from German fire behind a ridge in the Vercors area of southeastern France in February of 1944. At that time, the Resistance movements in the occupied countries of Western Europe were building toward a crescendo of activity in anticipation of an Allied invasion.

THE RESISTANCE

SIX BATTLEFIELDS OF THE RESISTANCE

During the spring and early summer of 1940, Denmark, Luxembourg, the Netherlands, Belgium, Norway and France (left) fell to Hitler's invading armies. In each country, small underground groups launched seemingly hopeless struggles against the mighty forces of the German Occupation. But as the various resistance networks expanded and grew increasingly skilled at sabotage and guerrilla harassment, their cumulative activities started to take on strategic importance, pinning down hundreds of thousands of German troops and greatly diminishing the benefits that Germany could expect from the factories, farms and resources of the occupied countries.

In France (right), the efforts of underground groups to unify were hampered by heavily guarded internal borders that were created by German partitioning. The Germans occupied the northern two thirds of the nation, annexing Alsace and Lorraine outright and forbidding movement into and out of a zone in the industrial north. The southern third of the country was governed from Vichy by a puppet regime until November 1942, when German forces took direct control to meet the threat posed by the Allied invasion of North Africa. Italy occupied part of southeastern France until September 1943, when the Allied invasion forces knocked Italy out of the War.

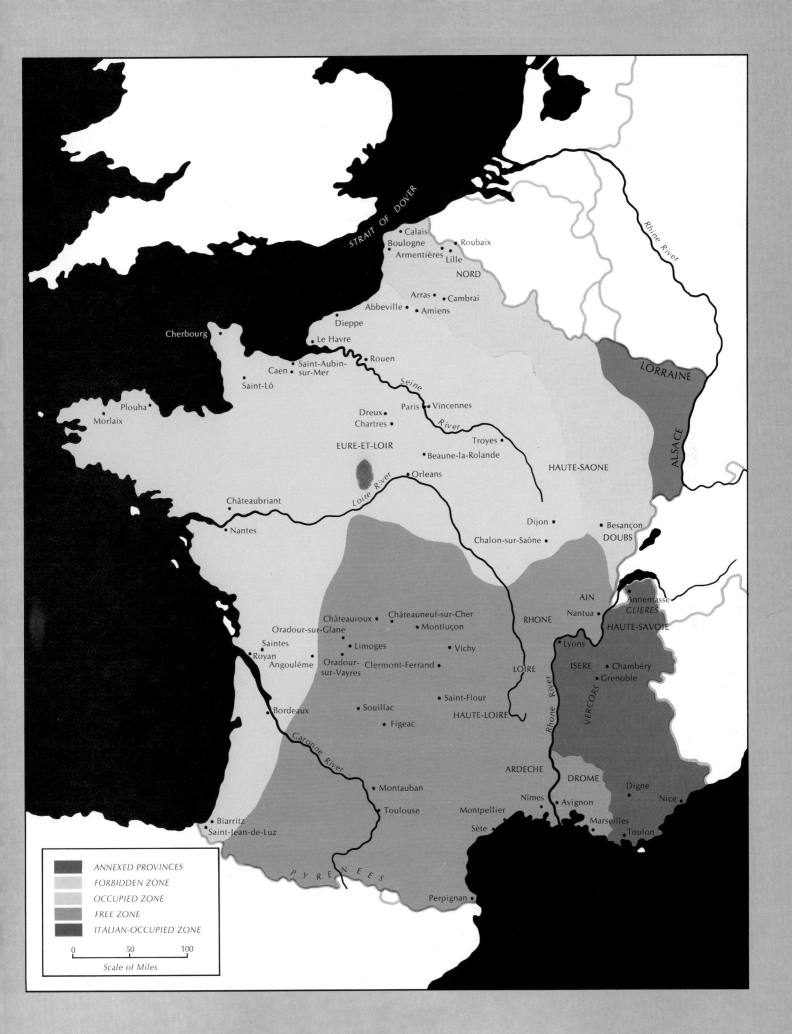

STRAIT OF DOVER

Rhine River

• Calais
Boulogne •
Armentières • • Roubaix
• Lille

NORD

Arras • • Cambrai
Abbeville • • Amiens

• Dieppe

Cherbourg •

• Le Havre

LORRAINE

Saint-Aubin-
sur-Mer • • Rouen
Caen •

Saint-Lô •

Seine

Plouha •

Paris • • Vincennes
Dreux •
Chartres •

River

ALSACE

Morlaix •

• Troyes

EURE-ET-LOIR

• Beaune-la-Rolande

HAUTE-SAONE

• Orléans

Loire River

Châteaubriant •

• Dijon

• Besançon

• Nantes

Chalon-sur-Saône •

DOUBS

AIN
• Annemasse
Nantua • GLIERES

Châteauroux • • Châteauneuf-sur-Cher
Oradour-sur-Glane • • Montluçon
Saintes •
• Royan • Limoges
Angoulême • Oradour- • Clermont-Ferrand
sur-Vayres

RHONE

HAUTE-SAVOIE

Lyons •

ISERE • Chambéry
• Grenoble

• Vichy

LOIRE

VERCORS

• Saint-Flour

• Souillac
• Figeac

HAUTE-LOIRE

Bordeaux •

Garonne River

ARDECHE

DROME

• Digne
• Nice

• Montauban

Nîmes •
• Avignon

• Toulouse
Montpellier •

Marseilles •
• Toulon

Biarritz •
Saint-Jean-de-Luz •

Sète •

P Y R E N E E S

Perpignan •

▮ ANNEXED PROVINCES
▮ FORBIDDEN ZONE
▮ OCCUPIED ZONE
▮ FREE ZONE
▮ ITALIAN-OCCUPIED ZONE

0   50   100

Scale of Miles

WORLD WAR II · TIME-LIFE BOOKS · ALEXANDRIA, VIRGINIA

BY RUSSELL MILLER
AND THE EDITORS OF TIME-LIFE BOOKS

THE RESISTANCE

Time-Life Books Inc.
is a wholly owned subsidiary of
TIME INCORPORATED

Founder: Henry R. Luce 1898-1967

Editor-in-Chief: Henry Anatole Grunwald
Chairman of the Board: Andrew Heiskell
President: James R. Shepley
Vice Chairmen: Roy E. Larsen, Arthur Temple
Editorial Director: Ralph Graves

TIME-LIFE BOOKS INC.

Managing Editor: Jerry Korn
Executive Editor: David Maness
Assistant Managing Editors: Dale M. Brown
(planning), George Constable, Jim Hicks (acting),
Martin Mann, John Paul Porter
Art Director: Tom Suzuki
Chief of Research: David L. Harrison
Director of Photography: Robert G. Mason
Senior Text Editor: Diana Hirsh
Assistant Art Director: Arnold C. Holeywell
Assistant Chief of Research: Carolyn L. Sackett
Assistant Director of Photography: Dolores A. Littles

Chairman: Joan D. Manley
President: John D. McSweeney
Executive Vice Presidents: Carl G. Jaeger,
John Steven Maxwell, David J. Walsh
Vice Presidents: Peter G. Barnes (comptroller),
Nicholas Benton (public relations), John L. Canova
(sales), Nicholas J. C. Ingleton (Asia),
James L. Mercer (Europe/South Pacific),
Herbert Sorkin (production), Paul R. Stewart
(promotion)
Personnel Director: Beatrice T. Dobie
Consumer Affairs Director: Carol Flaumenhaft

WORLD WAR II

Editorial Staff for The Resistance
Editor: Gerald Simons
Picture Editor/Designer: Raymond Ripper
Text Editors: Lydia Preston, Henry Woodhead
Staff Writers: Dalton Delan, Kumait Jawdat,
Tyler Mathisen, Brian McGinn,
Teresa M. C. R. Pruden
Chief Researcher: Oobie Gleysteen
Researchers: Kristin Baker, Loretta Y. Britten,
Mary G. Burns, Charlie Clark, Frances R. Glennon,
Chadwick Gregson, Clara Nicolai, Judy Shanks,
Jean Strong
Art Assistant: Mary Louise Mooney
Editorial Assistant: Connie Strawbridge

Editorial Production
Production Editor: Douglas B. Graham
Operations Manager: Gennaro C. Esposito,
Gordon E. Buck (assistant)
Assistant Production Editor: Feliciano Madrid
Quality Control: Robert L. Young (director),
James J. Cox (assistant), Michael G. Wight
(associate)
Art Coordinator: Anne B. Landry
Copy Staff: Susan B. Galloway (chief),
Peter Kaufman, Victoria Lee, Celia Beattie
Picture Department: Alvin L. Ferrell
Traffic: Jeanne Potter

Correspondents: Elisabeth Kraemer (Bonn);
Margot Hapgood, Dorothy Bacon, Lesley Coleman
(London); Susan Jonas, Lucy T. Voulgaris (New
York); Maria Vincenza Aloisi, Josephine du Brusle
(Paris); Ann Natanson (Rome). Valuable assistance
was also provided by: Wibo van de Linde
(Amsterdam); Brigid Grauman, Chris Redman
(Brussels); Karin Hills, Sandy Jacobi (Copenhagen);
Robert Slater (Jerusalem); Carolyn T. Chubet,
Miriam Hsia (New York); Dag Christensen (Oslo);
M. T. Hirschkoff (Paris).

The Author: RUSSELL MILLER is a freelance writer
and journalist based in London. A former officer in
the British Army, he has been a regular contributor
to The Sunday Times, and his work is syndicated
throughout the world.

The Consultants: COLONEL JOHN R. ELTING, USA
(Ret.), is a military historian and author of The
Battle of Bunker's Hill, The Battles of Saratoga and
Military History and Atlas of the Napoleonic Wars.
He edited Military Uniforms in America: The Era
of the American Revolution, 1755-1795 and Mili-
tary Uniforms of America: Years of Growth, 1796-
1851, and was associate editor of The West Point
Atlas of American Wars.

M. R. D. FOOT was a British Army major in World
War II who served as a parachutist with Special Air
Service and received the French Croix de Guerre
for service with the Resistance in Brittany. He
taught politics and history at Oxford, was Professor
of Modern History at the University of Manchester, edited the Gladstone Diaries, and is the author
of SOE in France, Resistance and Six Faces of Courage; he is co-author of MI 9.

Library of Congress Cataloging in Publication Data

Miller, Russell.
  The resistance.

  (World War II; v. 17)
  Bibliography: p.
  Includes index.
  1. World War, 1939-1945—Underground move-
ments—Europe. I. Time-Life Books. II. Title. III. Series.
D802.E9M54   940.53'4   79-14316
ISBN 0-8094-2524-6
ISBN 0-8094-2523-8 lib. bdg.

CONTENTS

FIRST ACTS OF DEFIANCE

Defying the Germans' ban on tributes to Belgium's World War I Unknown Soldier, the old veteran in charge of the tomb sneaks flowers past Brussels policemen.

A FROSTY RECEPTION FOR THE CONQUERORS

Between April and June of 1940, German armies overran six nations of Western Europe: Denmark, Norway, Luxembourg, Holland, Belgium and France. The citizens of these countries were left stunned, frightened and leaderless. They expected nothing but humiliation and exploitation at German hands, and it seemed foolhardy to resist.

Nevertheless, resistance began almost at once in all of the occupied countries. It was not organized, militant action; that would take months to develop. Rather, it was passive resistance, mostly spur-of-the-moment: Individuals showed their patriotism in any small way they could. "Travelers on the metro would deliberately direct Germans to stations miles out of their way," Frenchwoman Lucie Aubrac wrote of Paris; "bus conductors would skip stops where Germans wanted to get off." In much the same vein, citizens in Amsterdam left cafés when a German soldier entered, and they quit patronizing shops that posted signs saying "German spoken here."

At first only a few people defied the Germans openly, and their reactions tended to be more hot-tempered than calculated. A Danish innkeeper, for example, was so enraged when his flag was replaced by a swastika that he pulled down the entire flagpole. The Germans erected a new flagpole, whereupon the innkeeper set up the old one again and hoisted an enormous new Danish flag *(right)*. Then he triumphantly told the German sentry, "Now you can guard this one too!"

Resistance of this sort prompted Madame Aubrac to observe that the French behaved "a little like children in the presence of a boorish teacher." But the spontaneous gestures of resentful patriots had a double-barreled effect. They denied the full fruits of victory to the German troops and, in time, helped to weaken their discipline and resolve. And no matter how petty, these acts of resistance fortified the conquered peoples in the dark early days of their long ordeal. Said one fiery French resistant, "It is this ludicrous little thing—this refusal to submit—that saved our human dignity."

Defying a shutdown of Norway's school system, an instructor holds classes at home. Schools were closed when teachers refused to join a Nazi union.

The Danish national flag flies beside the swastika with the grudging permission of the Germans, who were trying to win the cooperation of the vanquished Danes.

TALKING WALLS AND SYMBOLS OF VICTORY

One of the first signs of public antipathy toward the German occupiers was the seditious handiwork of graffiti artists. For the most part, these patriots struck under cover of darkness, each night leaving a new crop of anti-German slogans and symbols for the scrutiny of countrymen on their way to work the next day. In Norway, patriots decorated walls and billboards with the initials of their King, Haakon VII, who had fled the country rather than submit to German rule. In France the most popular symbol of resistance was the double-barred cross of Lorraine, adopted by the London-based leader of the Free French, General Charles de Gaulle.

One symbol was used in all the occupied countries to invoke the day when the people would again be free—the V-for-Victory sign that came to be identified with that stubborn fighter, British Prime Minister Winston S. Churchill. The letter V was carved on trees, scratched on coins, painted on cars, scrawled on walls and used to deface propaganda posters put up by the Germans.

Frenchmen frequently combined the V with the cross of Lorraine *(left)*. On one such poster, a Parisian exhorted passersby to "make a stroke for de Gaulle." Fellow patriots followed his bidding and made row upon row of pencil marks signaling their allegiance to the general. The Germans cut out the marks, but the holes only increased the effect.

These furtive acts of patriotism were not enough for some citizens. At the risk of a heavy fine or even imprisonment, they worked various symbols of resistance into their jewelry and articles of clothing and wore them publicly *(pages 14-15)* to taunt the Germans.

In a picture sequence made by a Resistance photographer to document the resolve of ordinary citizens, a nocturnal graffiti artist in Paris rips down a German propaganda poster and crayons in its place the slogan "Vive de Gaulle." To the left, he scrawls a V-for-Victory sign and places inside it a cross of Lorraine, the emblem of a border region that France got back from Germany after World War I.

POPULATIONS abandonnées, *faites confiance* AU SOLDAT ALLEMAND!

Replying bitterly to a propaganda poster of a German soldier protecting French children, a citizen scrawled: "He replaces the father he killed."

The house of a Belgian collaborator was surreptitiously splashed with paint by irate patriots, identifying the traitor and holding him up to public scorn.

In a photograph that was smuggled out of Norway, two courageous patriots assemble a stone graffito: the monogram of their escaped King Haakon VII.

A pair of sunbathing Norwegians proclaim their patriotism in lipstick: "Down with N.S." (the Nazi Party in Norway) and the monogram of King Haakon VII.

Vexed by a provocative cap knit in the image of the Royal Air Force bull's-eye emblem, a German soldier (left) orders a Copenhagen girl's name recorded.

A jockey at Paris' Longchamps racetrack sports a huge cross of Lorraine in June 1940, before the Germans realized that the cross was a symbol of resistance.

Interrupting a German military review, an elderly Parisian deliberately crosses in front of the line of soldiers, forcing a police officer to reroute her (inset).

BRAZEN AFFRONTS TO THE OCCUPATION

Boldly or on the sly, many ordinary citizens went out of their way to annoy and insult the German troops.

In Paris, a blind beggar taunted the Germans by playing the "Marseillaise" on his accordion. An old lady made a practice of tripping soldiers with her cane. In Dutch theaters, citizens walked out when Nazi propaganda films began—until a German law forbade such early departures. Danes talked back to propaganda films. "Who is that man?" was a facetious response when the Führer appeared on screen. After an announcer's portentous comment, "Here are 100 bombers on their way to attack England," the theater rang with a gibe at exaggerated German battle claims: "Two hundred bombers returned."

The Germans were well aware that such remarks were not offered in jest, and increasingly their nerves were frayed by the resentment and contempt that they felt all around them.

A daring Dutchman strolls naked through the streets of Amsterdam to protest strict German clothes rationing.

On his daily ride through Copenhagen, King Christian X is stirred by the greetings of his patriotic subjects.

A Danish youngster pauses at the site of a German reprisal execution.

EARLY OUTBREAKS OF PATRIOTIC VIOLENCE

By the fall of 1940, local opposition to the Occupation was hardening, and more and more citizens were venting their hatred for Hitler's new order. In Bordeaux, seamen spat at German officers and paid for doing so with a year in jail. The Dutch pro-Nazi National Socialists said that on a march through a working-class district of Rotterdam "it rained tiles and flowerpots and some other unmentionable household articles, with contents."

Some daring patriots became amateur saboteurs. A Frenchman cut German telephone lines; he was executed by firing squad. A young Dane, undaunted by the death penalty for sabotage, used incendiary bombs made of sugar, acid and calcium chlorate to destroy German staff cars. More important, many freelance patriots began joining forces, working against the Germans on an organized basis. With the spread of these militant groups, the Resistance finally came of age.

At the risk of being shot on sight, Dutch patriots spread a large flag beside a

canal in Amsterdam where 29 countrymen had been killed by the Germans. They were executed in reprisal for a Dutch attempt to assassinate the local SS chief.

1

Shortly before 6 o'clock on the evening of June 18, 1940, an obscure French general sat down at a microphone in Studio B2 at the British Broadcasting Company in London and prepared to broadcast to his nation, which lay prostrate before the invading German armies. The general was an intimidating figure of a man: immensely tall, formidably straight and stiff, with a haughty manner that was somehow emphasized by his large nose and drooping eyelids. His name was Charles de Gaulle.

The employees of the BBC did not know very much about de Gaulle beyond the fact that he had gotten permission from Prime Minister Winston Churchill to make the broadcast. They were aware that he had only recently been promoted to the rank of general, and that he had arrived from France just the day before, leaving in the nick of time as German armored columns rolled into Paris. The employees who had come into contact with de Gaulle said that he acted very much as if he had just won a war; he was almost dictatorial in his demands.

Under the circumstances, de Gaulle's arrogance was more than a little annoying to his British hosts. France, in spite of its much-vaunted military might, had collapsed in the face of Hitler's armies in less than six weeks. And the fall of France had marked the completion of two apocalyptic months for the democracies of western Europe; five other countries—Denmark, Norway, Holland, Luxembourg and Belgium—had already succumbed to Hitler's latest blitzkrieg. England, now completely stripped of allies, was itself in dire peril of a German invasion, and the British had neither the time nor the patience for lectures from a failed French general who presumed, without authority, to act as his nation's leader-in-exile.

When a green light went on in the studio to signal that he was on the air, de Gaulle cleared his throat and began to speak in impassioned tones. "It is quite true that we were, and still are, overwhelmed by enemy mechanized forces, both on the ground and in the air. . . . Must we abandon all hope? Is our defeat final and irremediable? To those questions I answer—No!"

De Gaulle exhorted his fellow countrymen to join him and to work toward their own liberation. He reminded them that France's overseas empire was still free, that Great Britain was still fighting and that there were other mighty

THE SHADOW WAR BEGINS

forces that had not yet been brought into play. "There still exists in the world everything we need to crush our enemies one day. . . .

"Whatever happens, the flame of French resistance must not and shall not be extinguished."

In time, those brave words would prove to be a prophecy without a single flaw. Two great powers that were then noncombatants, the United States and the Soviet Union, would join the war against Hitler's Germany, and eventually they would turn the tide of victory. Until their prodigious manpower and matériel were brought to bear, the Allied cause would be sustained by the British and by growing resistance inside France and the other occupied countries of Western Europe.

France, as de Gaulle realized, was the key to successful resistance against Germany. It was the most populous and the most heavily industrialized of the six occupied countries. Without exploiting French economic resources to the fullest, Germany would steadily lose ground in a lengthening war of attrition. Furthermore, France was strategically vital to the liberation of Europe; its proximity to Britain and its largely open countryside—suitable for tank movements—made it the natural place for an invasion by Germany's enemies.

It would take time for resistance in France and in the other occupied countries to mature. Not until 1942 at the earliest would the scattered, tentative underground groups within any country merge to form a unified opposition to the occupiers. Not until then would resistance become the Resistance—an organized movement capable of playing a real role in the War. Even then, the Resistance throughout Europe would remain a series of separate national operations, only loosely coordinated by the various Allied intelligence agencies.

But in each country, the Resistance groups would multiply and expand their activities, gathering and relaying intelligence to London, organizing and executing sabotage on an ever grander scale, helping thousands of people to escape from the occupied countries. Their myriad acts of defiance and destruction would ultimately become a conflagration in 1944, when the Allied armies in England prepared to reinvade the European continent. Then, thanks in large measure to widespread Resistance activity, the Allies would be able to win their foothold in France without having to face some 50 German divisions, which were pinned down in out-of-the-way sections of France and in the other occupied countries of Western Europe.

Yet on the warm June night when de Gaulle addressed his nation, the mere suggestion of resistance seemed to be pure rhetoric—an exercise in wishful thinking. Very few people in France heard de Gaulle's radio speech, and even fewer heeded his call.

On the dusty roads leading south from Paris, the demoralized remnants of the French Army joined streams of panic-stricken citizens fleeing from the advancing German forces. The refugees had packed the belongings they were taking with them on anything that would move—cars, taxis, trucks, carts, bicycles, wheelbarrows, baby carriages. Many tied mattresses to the roofs of the automobiles as protection against machine-gunning from the air.

In towns and villages on the roads south, the refugees crowded the hotels and cafés, besieged the gasoline pumps and spread their fear like a contagion to families who had not thought of abandoning their homes. At the peak of the exodus, as many as 10 million Frenchmen clogged the roadways. They left shops unstaffed, production lines unmanned, crops untended, cows unmilked, and houses unlocked and deserted.

The French people were stunned and shamed by the events of May and June 1940. It was inconceivable to them that their nation, with its long and glorious military heritage, could have been conquered so quickly and so easily. It was inconceivable but true. Their Army had been smashed, and now all was lost.

Overwhelmed by the catastrophe, they turned for support and guidance to an 84-year-old soldier whose main claim to political leadership rested on a reputation he had gained a quarter of a century before during the First World War. Marshal Henri Philippe Pétain, the hero of the Battle of Verdun, took over as Prime Minister on the 17th of June. That same day, he broadcast to the nation in a quavering voice "I give to France the gift of my person to alleviate her misfortunes. . . . With a heavy heart I tell you today that the fighting must stop."

"The tone of his homily made me want to retch," recalled

author Simone de Beauvoir. "All the same, I was relieved to hear the shedding of French blood would cease at last."

The relief that came with the armistice was almost universal among the French. The old soldier—proud, erect, his pale blue eyes bright and confident—was hailed as a savior who could rescue France from the abyss of war and restore order in the chaotic nation. Soon a cult grew up around the "sacred person" of the venerable marshal. His picture—in uniform, of course—appeared everywhere, in shops and offices, on posters in the streets, on souvenir cups and plates, on flags, behind official desks. There was no escaping his kindly, paternal stare. New books about such heroic figures as Napoleon, Louis XIV and Joan of Arc made a point of stressing amazing similarities with the marshal. Songs were written in adoration ("Marshal, here we are, we your children, standing before you . . ."); prayers were rewritten to praise him (". . . And deliver us from evil, O Marshal of France").

The armistice that Pétain called for was signed on June 22 in the historic railway carriage in the forest of Compiègne, where France's Marshal Foch had dictated terms to the defeated Germans in 1918. Under Hitler's terms, two thirds of France was to be occupied and governed by the German Army (map, page 3), and the cost of this service—set at a staggering 400 million francs (approximately nine million dollars) per day—was to be paid entirely by the French. Nearly two million French soldiers were deported to various prison camps, stripping France of the core of its labor force.

Still, it could have been worse. A large part of southern France was to be left unoccupied, and this supposedly free sector would serve as a sanctuary for the oppressed and for the refugee legions on the road. In the light of what little was known about the cruel fate of German-occupied countries to the east, the French in the unoccupied zone could consider themselves comparatively lucky.

Marshal Pétain established his government at Vichy, a spa in the unoccupied zone about 175 miles south of Paris, and

French servicemen who fled their country wait to sign up as members of a French combat unit in a London recruiting office in July of 1940. The force, formed shortly after the fall of France, was the nucleus of a Free French army that numbered well over 100,000 men four years later.

he promptly adopted a policy of collaboration with the Germans that went so far as to embrace the tenets of Nazi anti-Semitism. A few days after meeting Hitler at Montoire-sur-le-Loire in October, the marshal again broadcast to the nation. "It is in a spirit of honor, and to maintain the unity of France," he declared, ". . . that I enter today upon the path of collaboration."

By and large, people in the unoccupied zone took a pragmatic attitude toward collaboration: like it or not, it was the price they had to pay for keeping the abominable Germans out. However, the Frenchmen in the larger zone that was occupied were discovering to their surprise that the German troops were very different from the ogres they had previously been painted. They seemed to be polite and decent men. And the German authorities showed unexpected signs of humanity; for one thing, they opened soup kitchens in Paris to tide over the hungry populace until the disrupted food supply from the countryside was flowing again. So once the initial terror had been dispelled, many citizens in the occupied zone resigned themselves to accepting the conquerors.

Many went beyond mere acceptance. In a letter to her son, a woman living in Saintes, north of Bordeaux, wrote admiringly that "the population gave the victors a hearty welcome, the girls waving their handkerchiefs and scarves at the athletic young men on motorcycles, handsome as gods, with laughter in their eyes."

The Frenchmen of the north, being ruled directly by the German military, were not obliged to embrace Vichy's collaborationist policy. But many did, some because it seemed to be the way to keep the peace secure, others so that they might profit by the German presence. Jean Bruller, later renowned as a Resistance writer under the pseudonym Vercors, deplored the unpatriotic venality and complacence of his neighbors in a village east of Paris. "I could not help realizing that the villagers, beginning with my own employer, were quite unruffled by the occupier's presence," Vercors wrote. "The farmer's wife went one better: she made

Prime Minister Winston S. Churchill escorts the grim-faced leader of the Free French, General Charles de Gaulle, on an inspection tour of a tank unit in Britain in March of 1941. Although Churchill supported de Gaulle's resistance movement, he was frequently exasperated by the imperious Frenchman. The Prime Minister was quoted as saying: "The heaviest cross I have to bear is the Cross of Lorraine"—the symbol of liberation that General de Gaulle had adopted as his own.

the most of it quite shamelessly, letting her customers, her neighbors and even her own relatives go without milk, butter and eggs that she could sell to the Germans at a higher price.

"Things were not much different in Paris, I felt. The Opéra and the Comédie-Française were playing to stalls packed with officers in full-dress uniforms. The cafés were crowded with shaven square skulls and Frenchmen unconcernedly drinking cheek by jowl. In the automobile-less streets, German soldiers, smartly dressed Frenchwomen and corpulent businessmen let themselves be towed in cycle cabs, there being no taxis. I could not bear the sight of my own fellow creatures reduced to beasts of burden, even with their own consent to this degradation."

By the autumn of 1940, it had become all too clear to patriotic Frenchmen that their road to resistance would be a long and hard one.

In the wake of the blitzkrieg, conditions in the other occupied nations of Western Europe seemed hardly more conducive to resistance. In all five countries, the citizens were left stunned, unorganized, disenfranchised and fearing the worst. They too sought first to find a way to survive, which for most people meant obeying the edicts of the Occupation. Yet, underlying their conformity, the citizens of these countries had certain intangible assets the French lacked that came to the fore readily as the shock of defeat wore off.

Three of the countries—Denmark, Holland and Luxembourg—were calm in defeat partly because they had put little reliance on their small, weak armed forces. The citizens knew they would be helpless in the event of attack, and when it came, they were neither surprised nor demoralized by the Germans' easy triumph. The Norwegian and Belgian Armies had battled courageously before they succumbed, and the people retained their national pride in spite of their heavy casualties and their ultimate surrender.

As Belgium teetered on the brink of defeat, King Leopold III ordered his ministers to form a government-in-exile. They urged the King to leave, too, but he refused to desert his people. Leopold arranged the surrender of his shattered forces and declared himself a prisoner of war, refusing to bargain for concessions with the Germans.

The Belgian people were no strangers to resistance; many of them remembered the underground tactics they had used during four years of German occupation in the First World War. Now, despite the initial chaos in the country— nearly two million refugees clogged the roads—Belgian patriots quickly established a clandestine press. Soon dozens of underground newspapers were inveighing against the German occupiers, and numerous intelligence circuits were sending information to the government-in-exile in London.

Holland's government, too, left for exile in London, three days after the Germans attacked on May 10, 1940. With the ministers went their Queen, Wilhelmina, who had narrowly

King Haakon VII of Norway (foreground) and the heir to the throne, Crown Prince Olav, review free Norwegian troops at a training base in Scotland in 1943. The popular King frequently visited his exiled forces to help boost morale in anticipation of combat, but few of the troops ever saw action.

escaped a kidnap attempt by a company of German paratroopers. On May 14, facing a hopeless situation, the Dutch armed forces were ordered by their Commander in Chief to stop fighting, but thousands of troops refused to surrender to the Germans. Instead, many went into hiding, taking their weapons with them, and coolly waited for the day when they could strike a blow against the conquerors.

To prepare for that day, the Dutch quickly made capital of one of their principal industries: printing. Using the abundance of small presses in the country, many skilled printers began to publish anti-German books, newspapers and pamphlets in secret. On May 15, the day the Dutch armed forces officially surrendered, the first underground publication appeared. In time more than 1,000 illegal newspapers would circulate regularly in Holland, to the immense irritation of the German Occupation forces.

The Dutch kept up their morale with a persistent display of the ill will they bore the Germans. And the effect on German morale was considerable. Hugo Bleicher, a military policeman assigned to duty in The Hague in June 1940, later wrote: "We could see in Holland for the first time what foreigners thought of us in the occupied countries. The population regarded us with contemptuous aloofness and treated us as if we were not there. It was hard on the nerves to spend inactive months in the midst of a population that had only hatred and contempt for us."

The Dutch used the birthday of the Queen's son-in-law, Prince Bernhard, for an organized exhibition of patriotism. Thousands of citizens wore or carried Bernhard's favorite flower, a white carnation, in loyalty to the house of Orange. When German soldiers began snatching the flowers, a few brave souls slipped razor blades among the petals.

In Denmark, as in Holland, the citizens had quietly accepted defeat when the Germans occupied most of their country in a single day, April 9, 1940. The Danes were surprised and relieved to discover that Hitler, who considered their racial origins to be impeccably Aryan, had chosen them for preferential treatment—part of his plan to transform Denmark into what he called "his model protectorate." Their government remained in office; their shops did business without hindrance; their teachers taught unimpeded. The Danes punctiliously obeyed the order of their King, Christian X, to remain calm and behave "correctly" to the occupier. Foreign observers concluded that Denmark had become Germany's willing pawn, but the Germans soon discovered otherwise. What seemed to some to be correct behavior was in fact a cool, tough hostility. "To the Danes," said *The Times* of London, "belongs the credit of inventing a new order, unthought of by Hitler—the Order of the Cold Shoulder, D.K.S., standing for *Den Kolde Skulder*—and it expresses the feelings towards the Germans of about 90 per cent of the Danish population."

The cold shoulder was only the first sign of Danish resistance. There soon followed individual acts of sabotage and secret meetings that led to the formation of underground cells. In Copenhagen, a group of Danish staff officers established an intelligence-gathering network known as the Princes and began sending the British valuable information

Queen Wilhelmina of the Netherlands, who fled to Britain to establish a government-in-exile, broadcasts encouragement to her countrymen from London in 1942. To show her solidarity with her people, the Queen tried to greet personally every Dutchman who escaped to England, and she refused to eat foods that were unavailable or unaffordable in Holland.

on the disposition of German troops, planes and ships.

After Norway fell to the Germans in June 1940, King Haakon VII and his ministers made their way to London. Almost at once, the survivors of the crushed Norwegian Army met in small, furtive groups to map out avenues of resistance. In time, the groups formed an underground network known as Milorg. This force maintained close contact with the leaders in London and laid plans to seize control of their country in the event of an Allied invasion.

The overwhelming majority of Norwegians remained loyal to their government-in-exile. The patriots had no trouble whatever making up their minds about Vidkun Quisling, the pompous leader of Norway's Nazi Party, who appointed himself Prime Minister on April 12, three days after the invasion began. The Norwegians responded to Quisling's bluster with open ridicule: the upper classes snubbed him, labor leaders mocked him, public servants turned down his offers of high government posts. Quisling became such a laughingstock that the embarrassed Germans kicked him out of office six days later. He would make a comeback in 1942—by which time his name had entered the English language as a synonym for "traitor."

France was a much more complicated case: a nation split between right and left and thoroughly frustrated by decades of ineffectual government under the Third Republic. "Yes, long before the War," wrote novelist André Gide, "France stank of defeat. She was already falling apart to such a degree that perhaps the only thing that could save her was—*is* perhaps—this very disaster in which to retemper her energies." Many Frenchmen saw Vichy as a revolutionary government that would meet the nation's need for radical reform. "Reform is in the air," said a judge in Rouen, in the occupied zone. Said a professor on the faculty at Montpellier, in southern France, "The National Revolution has done in one year what the former regime failed lamentably to do in more than a century."

On the whole, the French people agreed. Disillusionment, apathy and, in some quarters, outright disdain for the former leadership were common among the electorate. The decade of the 1930s had been marked by growing tension and polarization between the political extremes. A declining economy, social distress, financial scandal and foreign-

policy crises had undermined successive administrations. With the disintegration of the Popular Front at home and the government's apparent weakness in dealing with the growing threat from abroad, the Third Republic had been left with few supporters within the country.

So Frenchmen of various shades of Rightist persuasion united behind Pétain. Some Leftists joined them, on the convenient theory that the marshal was playing a "double game," and that when the time was right he would show his hand, eject his home-grown Nazis and take dramatic steps to liberate the occupied territory.

But many Leftists, together with many apolitical people who still clung to their nation's traditional enmity for Germany, possessed a burning desire to resist the Occupation. And in spite of their lack of a framework for organized resistance, they began, in desultory fashion, to resist.

The first stirrings of French opposition were, like those in the other occupied countries, little more than a show of dumb insolence that usually provided more satisfaction for the individual than anxiety for the occupier. The mayor of a town in the Paris area stopped the town-hall clock to show that he did not recognize the "new times." In Alsace-Lorraine, where the authorities fined citizens for speaking French, a woman walked into a government office, said a cheery "Bonjour" and then paid the fine twice, remarking: "That's for the next time." In a photographer's shopwindow at the Place d'Italie in Paris, a large photograph of Pétain was prominently displayed with the label "Sold." Such incidents might have produced no more than a surreptitious smirk, but they were important nevertheless. They lowered the status of the occupier, encouraged further wary defiance and bolstered the morale of the people in the face of national humiliation.

At the beginning, the Germans refused to be baited; vicious reprisals for defiance were to come later. Well into the fall of 1940 the occupiers continued to do their best to mollify the French and enlist their cooperation. They tried to soothe wounded pride by showing respect for French culture: Exhibitions were mounted, eminent French intellectuals were invited to visit Germany, lectures were organized and soldiers were ordered to take time to "meet the people," reassure the population of their good intentions and dispel the rumor that they cut off children's hands.

But increasing French defiance was not a problem that the Germans could solve simply with winning ways. Word of de Gaulle's broadcast from London had spread, and his name slowly came to represent opposition to the Occupation. Stickers imprinted with the slogan "Vive de Gaulle" appeared on the streets, in telephone booths, in railroad and subway stations, in public lavatories and even, on rare but uplifting occasions, on the back of German staff cars, planted there by some adventurous soul when the vehicle stopped at a traffic light.

Patriots decorated their watch chains, key rings and necklaces with the cross of Lorraine, a symbol of liberation to the French since the Crusades and a taunting reminder to the Occupation troops of Germany's defeat in World War I. (The duchy of Lorraine, taken from France in the Franco-Prussian War, was returned to France under the Versailles Treaty in 1919.) German signs were altered: *Offen* (open) became *Hoffen* (hope); *Raucher* (smoking compartment) became *Rache* (revenge). When French flags, forbidden by the Germans, were taken down by the French police, they were immediately hoisted again. Flowers were laid at monuments to national heroes.

Many Frenchmen were won over to resistance by Jean Texcier, a Socialist writer and journalist, who in August of 1940 had begun distributing a subversive pamphlet entitled "Advice to the Occupied." Written in simple, direct prose, it contained 33 separate counsels on how to behave toward the Germans. "Have no illusions: They are not tourists, they are conquerors. . . . You do not know their language or you have forgotten it. If one of them speaks to you in German, shrug helplessly and go quietly on your way. . . . If your haberdasher puts up a notice 'German spoken,' patronize the shop next door." Texcier's last suggestion was that the reader make copies of the pamphlet and pass them on. By this means, "Advice to the Occupied" was circulated widely throughout Paris. It could be found crumpled up in a ball on benches in the metro, or tucked into the crease of a cinema seat, or beneath an ashtray in a café, or just blowing along in the gutter.

The steady increase of French insults and taunts was irksome enough to the occupier, but the first isolated episodes of violence—sabotage, assaults on German soldiers and even an occasional killing—were truly disturbing. In Abbeville, near the Channel coast, someone shot a German with a Belgian 7.65 pistol every month for four months without ever being found. In the Doubs, a department near the Swiss border, rifle shots were fired at a German lieutenant. In Paris, three sentries outside the offices of the German Naval commander were fired on.

To counter the spread of anti-German activity, the Occupation authorities responded at first with fines. The going penalty was about 10,000 francs for the popular practice of defacing a propaganda poster. If the culprit was found to be a child (as was often the case), the parents could be arrest-

ed. Sabotage drew much heavier penalties—imprisonment for the perpetrators and a fine of up to seven million francs on a town where the crime took place. But Frenchmen persisted in cutting military telephone cables, which was highly satisfying and relatively easy.

As the number of such incidents increased, so did the severity of the punishment. In September, the resistance acquired a martyr when Pierre Roch, a 19-year-old sheet-metal worker from Royan in western France, was summarily executed for cutting a military cable. The occupiers also began to arrest protesters, many of whom were held as hostages to be readily available for execution in case of further violence against Germans.

Yet defiance became more open than ever. November 11, 1940, the anniversary of the armistice ending World War I,

was publicly celebrated in Paris at the Arc de Triomphe in direct disobedience of a German edict. Thousands of students gathered in the Champs-Elysées, many of them flaunting the national colors in the form of red, white and blue flowers, which, conveniently, some Parisian florists had produced in large quantities for sale that day. As the demonstrators moved toward the Arc de Triomphe, they were joined by passersby and by people sitting in the sidewalk cafés. When some students climbed the Arc de Triomphe waving a stick in each hand, the crowd soon got the joke: the French phrase for "two sticks" is *deux gaules*, pronounced like the name de Gaulle. When the cry went up, *"Vive de Gaulle, vive de Gaulle,"* the Germans decided they had had enough. Troops moved in from surrounding streets and began to break up the crowds. Scuffles started everywhere and shots were fired. Many people were arrested or injured before the streets were cleared, and next day Paris was rife with rumors of what had happened. Various reports set the death toll at anywhere between five and 50. In fact, no one had been killed.

The effect of the demonstration on public opinion was considerable. It showed Frenchmen for the first time that there was a large body of real opposition to the Germans and, just as important, it enabled individuals of like mind to identify one another. After Armistice Day, people who had recognized neighbors in the crowd, sometimes to their mutual astonishment, knew whom they could trust. This was a particular comfort, for in the general atmosphere of suspicion and fear that followed the defeat and Occupation, it was difficult to know who one's friends were. Those French people who took Pétain's armistice seriously judged any form of resistance to be a breach of honor, and many of them considered it their public duty to inform the Germans about workmates or neighbors who had voiced anti-German feelings.

Henri Frenay, an escaped prisoner of war who was later to become one of the great Resistance leaders, knew that a risk

ANROPELSE.

Guddommelige forsyn bak ånders ledestjerner
og gode makters lysdrift som fører folkeslag
den dulgte vei fra mørke mot mål i fagre fjerner!

Skal vi vår kjerne kjenne
avmektig eller sterk
ved det som her skal hende:
et veldig vårens verk?

Til folkets indre styrke, dets marg og motstandsevne
har vi vår lit å sette på prøvelsenes dag:
En brist i sjelens troskap — og alt skal rakne, revne!

Kom, lyse fortidsminner
i diktning, liv og dåd:
Når nuets livsmot svinner,
gi kraft og fremtidsråd!

Asker, 23. januar 1941.   Ragnar Hauger.

This poem, printed in the German-controlled Norwegian press, purports to praise the occupiers but uses an anagram to reveal the author's true allegiance. Read from top to bottom, the first letters of each line form the English sentence "God save the King"—referring to Norway's exiled King Haakon VII. English was widely understood among Norwegians, so the Resistance poet could expect many of his readers to break the simple code.

of betrayal had to be run if the movement was ever to gain real strength. At Marseilles, in the unoccupied zone, he was busily recruiting and raising funds for an embryonic resistance group. "Whenever I met someone," he explained, "I would start the same conversation. I would sound out his feelings about England and Hitler's Germany. I would acquaint him with my personal conviction that Germany would lose the War. I would point out that Britain was fiercely resisting the Nazi onslaught and that sooner or later America would intervene in the conflict as surely as she had done in 1917. France could not remain outside the coming battle. She must gird herself for action. I would then pause to get my interlocutor's reaction. If it seemed sympathetic, I would go still further: 'Men are already gathering in the shadows. Will you join them?'"

Frenay discovered little enthusiasm for his ideas in 1940. "The general drift of French public opinion was profoundly disappointing. Aside from the few friends whom we recruited, there was not a hint of the spirit of revolt. People had made themselves comfortable in defeat just as they would have done in victory. Their principal and sometimes exclusive worry was food."

What Frenay did not know was that other people in other parts of the country were also trying to form resistance groups. At Vichy, an energetic Right-Winger by the name of Georges Loustaunau-Lacau was laying the foundations for Alliance, a clandestine intelligence circuit that would eventually involve about 3,000 people. Gilbert Renault, soon to be known as Colonel Rémy, was planning the organization of the Confrérie Notre-Dame, an underground network that would supply London with plans of Hitler's Atlantic Coast defenses before a single cubic yard of concrete had been poured. Telephone workers in Paris were already working on the problem of how to tap long-distance cables that linked the city with Berlin.

And in Paris' anthropological museum, the Musée de l'Homme, a small group of scholars, led by a naturalized Russian émigré named Boris Vildé, was writing and secretly distributing anti-German propaganda. In December, the Musée de l'Homme group produced a clandestine newspaper called *Résistance,* with an unequivocal appeal on the front page: "Resist! This is the cry that comes from the hearts of all of you who suffer from our country's disaster. This is the wish of all of you who want to do your duty."

Citizens who had been content to deface German posters were becoming more aggressive. By December the Germans had found it necessary to put stickers on all their posters, warning that damaging the poster "would be considered an act of sabotage and punished by the severest penalties." On Christmas Eve, 1940, they also plastered Paris with new posters announcing the execution of one Jacques Bonsergent, a young engineer, for striking a German soldier.

The pseudonymous writer Vercors, who believed Bonsergent to be the first resistance martyr, wrote: "Next morning I found the posters surrounded by flowers, like so many tombs. Little flowers of every kind, mounted on pins, had been stuck on the posters during the night—real flowers and artificial ones, paper pansies, celluloid roses, small French and British flags . . . right in the middle of the staid and stuffy Faubourg Saint-Germain! What must it be like in the working-class districts of Belleville, Saint-Denis? I gulped down tears of pain and joy—joy at the first ripple, perceived at last, under the flowers offered to her first martyr, throbbing through the invisible soul of my country."

Even so, the militant resistants were often more dangerous to themselves than to the Germans. They had no weapons, no underground experience and—as stubbornly independent Frenchmen—very little practice at cooperative enterprise. They knew they were always at the mercy of informers and constantly being hunted by a ruthless enemy with enormous resources and proven skill at tracking down and squashing opposition. They had the will; what they lacked was a way. But that was to be provided very soon by a hush-hush organization with headquarters in London.

THE CLANDESTINE PRESS

Risking imprisonment or even the firing squad, Dutch journalists staffing an underground newspaper type and edit their stories in a secret Amsterdam office.

"JOIN THE FIGHT FOR FREEDOM"

On April 9, 1940, the day German forces occupied the Danish town of Slagelse, a 17-year-old schoolboy named Arne Sejr composed and typed up 25 copies of what he called "Ten Commandments for the Danes," and slipped them into neighborhood mailboxes the following night. The recipients were urged to

> *Do worthless work for the Germans,*
> *Work slowly for the Germans,*
> *Destroy everything useful to the Germans,*
> *Join the fight for Denmark's freedom!*

Young Arne Sejr's crude but passionate broadside marked the beginning of the underground press, the earliest form of organized resistance in each of the countries of the occupied West. Everywhere, small groups of like-minded friends joined up to plan, write and distribute subversive literature. Most of their early efforts were typewritten or mimeographed, although some were hand-copied.

The publications differed widely. Many focused on local affairs—German injustices and Resistance successes. Others were the voices of political parties, which used them to recruit and educate resistants. (One Norwegian publication was devoted entirely to how-to instructions for saboteurs.) Still others, slower to develop, were the work of professional reporters and editors—illustrated magazines and daily newspapers with circulations of up to 100,000. By 1944 the underground press in many areas was more widely read than lawful publications, and fully 1,200 Resistance periodicals were being put out in both Holland and France.

As the underground press grew, so did German efforts to suppress it. Some 3,000 journalists were arrested in Norway alone; more than 200 were executed. In Holland 120 people who worked on a single paper, *Loyalty*, lost their lives. To minimize the danger, the writers, photographers and printers on a given publication habitually worked in separate offices and frequently were unknown to one another. Yet some photographers took grave risks to record Resistance activities *(opposite)* as a national heritage.

A sampling of the numerous and aggressive underground publications in the Netherlands includes the Calvinist Trouw (Loyalty), the Communist De Waarheid (The Truth) and the Royalist Je Maintiendrai (I Will Stand Fast).

While a companion keeps watch, a Dutch photographer for the underground press uses a hidden camera to snap a picture through a hole in her handbag.

GATHERING AND REPORTING THE NEWS

The underground press was more than a means of promoting the Resistance. Many papers were full-scale news-gathering operations that supplied readers with uncensored domestic and foreign news.

Facts for the stories came from secret contacts in government agencies and police departments, from tapped official telephone and teletype lines, from the editorial staffs of legal newspapers who leaked news they dared not publish, and from foreign radio broadcasts.

Eventually, some underground journalists pooled their resources and set up clandestine news organizations to distribute daily or weekly bulletins to subscribing papers. The illegal Danish news service Información was especially efficient, issuing as many as four confidential bulletins a day to a group of 254 papers.

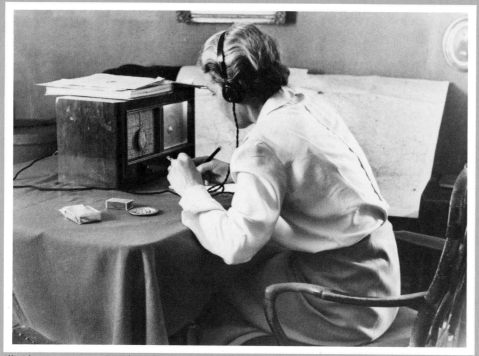

Illicitly monitoring a BBC broadcast, a Norwegian woman compiles the war news for an Oslo paper.

An Oslo typist transfers a reporter's draft to a mimeograph stencil. Typewriters, scarce and subject to seizure, were carefully hidden away when not in use.

An underground journalist edits a story in a temporary Amsterdam office. Editorial staffs of clandestine papers moved often to keep ahead of the Gestapo.

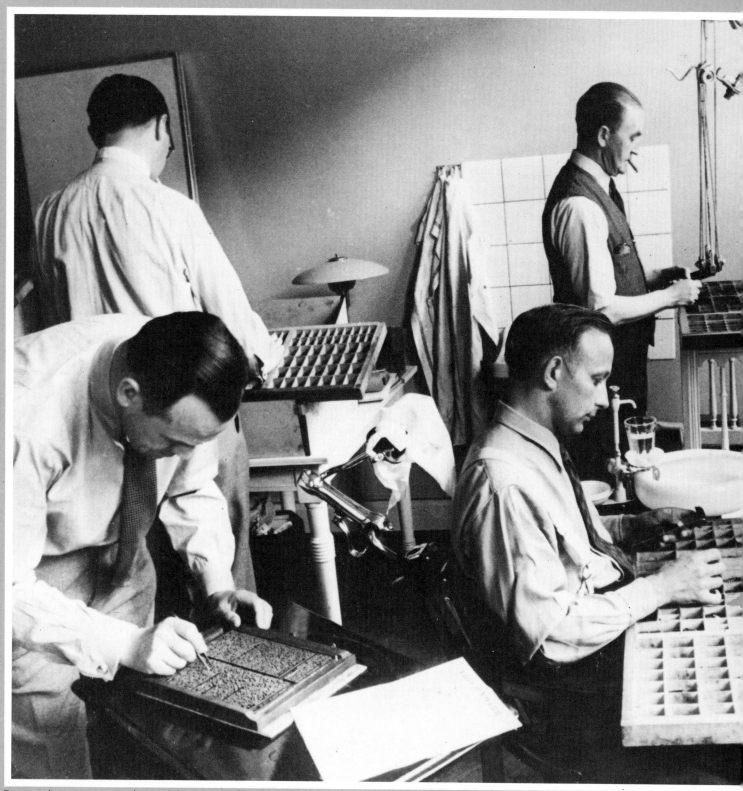

Typographers prepare an edition of the monthly Free Denmark in a dentist's office. In the event of a Gestapo raid, the trays of type and printing plates could b-

TEMPORARY QUARTERS, HIDDEN PRESSES

Once the news had been collected and written up, another set of dangers came into play: The news had to be mimeographed or printed, which required bulky equipment and materials that might easily attract unfriendly attention.

Small operations tucked their incriminating mimeograph machines and stocks of paper into secret compartments in attics, cellars and private apartments. One Dutch publisher set up his printing shop in a hollowed-out haystack. And Copenhagen's Informatión news service operated its mimeograph machine in a room at the government's medical research institute, behind a door rigged with a flashing red light that warned: "Dangerous Experiment in Progress."

Several large underground papers were run off at night on presses used for le-

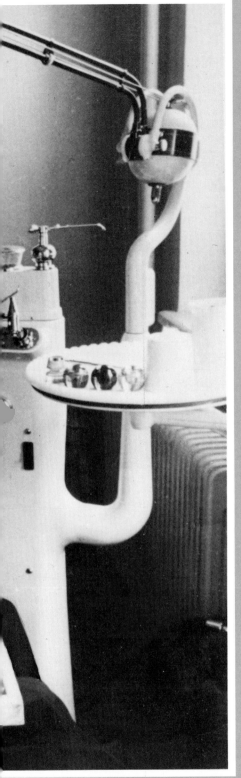

An armed guard takes a rest on a stack of paper while printers run off copies of The Free Danes.

oncealed inside secret cupboards within seconds.

Women collate a Norwegian underground paper in the basement of an Oslo apartment building.

gal publications by day. One underground group brazenly employed the same presses that were used for a Nazi-backed newspaper. Workers in the plant knew of the forbidden operation, but said nothing: resistants had promised them a nasty "professional accident" with "busy presses and molten lead" if they turned informer.

A woman messenger for a Dutch underground newspaper gathers mimeographed copies to distribute to subscribers in Amsterdam.

Another courier bicycles away from the printer's office with papers hidden in the bundles that are hanging from her handle bars.

SPREADING THE WORD IN BAGS AND SUITCASES

The trickiest part of any clandestine news operation was distributing copies of papers and journals to subscribers under the Germans' noses.

During the early years of the Occupation, many simple newssheets were sent out by mail in envelopes with bogus return addresses. But it was expensive and dangerous to mail publications with conspicuously large circulations. Most of the major papers were therefore delivered by messengers directly to the readers, sometimes by milkmen or mailmen who were resistants, but more often by women couriers who concealed copies in handbags, shopping bags, false-bottomed suitcases or in the clothing of their children.

In order to increase circulation, the papers advised readers to pass along their copies to someone else after they had finished with them. One Dutch paper urged readers who had a collector's instinct to resist the temptation to hoard newspaper copies; if they had to collect, it said, they might try German revolvers.

Pedestrians in Amsterdam read a copy of the Communist paper The Truth on a sidewalk kiosk. Though only a few thousand copies of The Truth were printed weekly, the actual readership was much larger, because of outdoor postings and distribution in factories, universities and well-populated areas where copies readily passed from hand to hand.

2

Peculiar doings on Baker Street
A franchise from Churchill to "set Europe ablaze"
SOE's simmering rivalry with de Gaulle
Bungled beginnings in occupied France
Coded nonsense from the BBC
Finishing school for secret operatives
A "safe house" becomes a "mousetrap"
The treacherous triple-agent called "La Chatte"
A house painter makes off with Hitler's defense plans
The Germans "play back" a captured transmitter
Major Giskes' April Fools' joke

HELP FROM BRITAIN

In the spring of 1941, a small metal plaque mounted outside 64 Baker Street in London—not far from the legendary chambers of Sherlock Holmes—announced to all that the building now housed the Inter-Services Research Bureau. The great detective no doubt would have been intrigued by so resonant yet unspecific a name—and doubtless he would have proceeded to demonstrate that the Inter-Services Research Bureau was just that and no more: a name.

Close observation would have revealed another peculiar establishment down the street, at No. 82. Most people entered and left the building through the back door, which opened onto a quiet and dilapidated mews. This was a strange way of doing business in what purported to be merely the administrative office of Marks and Spencer, a London department store.

The Baker Street addresses and their cover names concealed the operations of an extraordinary organization that its members irreverently called "the old firm" or "the racket." Its official title, known only to a few, was Special Operations Executive, or SOE. Every man and woman in its ranks was dedicated to a deadly serious undertaking: to wage clandestine warfare, through subversion and sabotage, in the occupied countries of Europe. It was a project that demanded the thickest veil of secrecy.

Even London's taxi drivers, who prided themselves on knowing what went on in the capital, never discovered the nature of the business conducted at the two establishments on Baker Street. Visitors were rarely received there, and recruits were interviewed in hotel rooms or in any of a number of London apartments rented by SOE for the purpose. And try as it might, the German secret service came no closer than the cabbies to finding the location of the London base for clandestine operations in Western Europe.

SOE had been founded by Prime Minister Churchill in the summer of 1940, when British fortunes were at their lowest ebb. In May the British Army had been shattered in the futile defense of France; only the heroic evacuation at Dunkirk in June had saved the remnants. Then, with the surrender of France on June 26, Britain lost her last important ally. The near future was expected to bring a German cross-Channel invasion, and Churchill and his ministers realized that years would pass before they could hope to mount a conventional military offensive against Germany in the occupied countries.

But there were unconventional ways of fighting back, and one of them was clandestine warfare, a subject that had long fascinated the Prime Minister. Now the exigencies of war directed Churchill's academic interest into practical application. "How wonderful it would be," he wrote in a memo to General Sir Hastings Ismay, his representative to the Chiefs of Staff, "if the Germans could be made to wonder where they were going to be struck next, instead of forcing us to try to wall in the island and roof it over!"

Toward this end, Churchill conceived of commando parties that would harass the Germans with hit-and-run raids, and of secret agents parachuted behind enemy lines to gather intelligence, conduct sabotage, train underground armies and sow the seeds of revolt among the occupied peoples. On July 19, the same day that a cocksure Hitler demanded that Britain surrender, the Prime Minister established the agency that would coordinate the underground war against Germany. He gave his brainchild an ambitious and dramatic mandate: "Set Europe ablaze."

Within three years' time, SOE would have a powerful and efficient network of underground agents in operation throughout Western Europe—and in Yugoslavia, Greece and the Middle East as well. Nonetheless, the organization was anything but an instant success. Indeed, its birth pains were severe enough to suggest that the new outfit might not make it out of the delivery room.

No sooner had Churchill informed his colleagues of his plans for SOE in 1940 than a bitter wrangle for control began. The War Office, the Foreign Office and the various British secret services all staked claims. Feelings ran so high at one point that when Lord Halifax stated his case on behalf of the Foreign Office, he was crustily told by Lord Lloyd, the Colonial Secretary, "You should never be consulted, because you would never consent to anything. You will never make a gangster." In the end, Churchill gave responsibility for SOE to Hugh Dalton, the energetic and creative Minister of Economic Warfare.

Unhappily, Dalton's appointment did not put an end to the acrimony. Many senior military officers looked with disdain upon any "irregular" operations, and they distrusted SOE from the start, labeling it amateurish, ungentlemanly and underhanded. This attitude went far to hamper SOE activities; the agency found it very difficult, for example, to persuade Royal Air Force commanders to assign one of their precious planes to transport a scruffy-looking individual to Europe on a mission no one would talk about. Petty bureaucrats, too, were offended by the unorthodox nature of an organization that operated under a cloak of secrecy and often treated regulations with cavalier disrespect.

To add to its problems, SOE found itself constantly contending with the haughty General de Gaulle and *his* secret service. In the early months of the War, as Churchill pointed out, "de Gaulle and his handful of followers could not claim to be an effective alternative French government." Britain had therefore continued relations with Marshal Pétain's Vichy government. To preserve this relationship, the British Foreign Office had insisted that SOE's French, or F, section operate independently of the general, and also that its activities in France be concealed from him. It was inevitable that de Gaulle would get wind of this, and it was just as inevitable that his reaction would be fury.

Dealings between the British and de Gaulle's followers became so strained that SOE was compelled to create an additional French section to work directly with de Gaulle's secret service. The primary objective of this joint effort was to foster a unified resistance movement in France. Meanwhile, the original F section continued its separate labors, concentrating on sabotage. The rivalry between the two SOE sections was intense, with each fervently believing the other to be inept.

De Gaulle's followers, generally called the Free French, were especially vexed at British attempts to poach on their countrymen and press them into intelligence service for Britain rather than for the homeland. "As soon as a Frenchman arrived in England," the general noted sourly in his memoirs, "he was invited to join the British Secret Services. It was only after a whole series of remonstrances and requests that he was allowed to join us. If, however, he had yielded, he was kept away from us and we would never see him."

The first attempts to send underground agents to France from Britain seemed to bear out the charges of rank amateurism leveled at both SOE and the Free French. Two of de Gaulle's agents, equipped with carrier pigeons to convey their intelligence reports back to England, paddled a rubber dinghy ashore at Saint Aubin in Normandy on the night of August 4, 1940, and promptly disappeared. It was assumed they had been either arrested or shot—until they showed up again in London at the beginning of 1941 and explained what had happened. The area in which they had landed was so heavily patrolled by German soldiers that they had been obliged to hide their cumbersome pigeon basket to escape. They were never able to retrieve it, and consequently had abandoned the mission.

SOE fared no better in its early efforts. An attempt to land a group of three agents by motor torpedo boat on the coast of Brittany near Morlaix on the night of August 1, 1940, was aborted when the boat encountered a German coastal convoy. On the night of November 14, the first SOE agent assigned to parachute into France arrived over the target area in Brittany and then, succumbing to a sudden case of nerves, refused to jump.

In fact, the infant organization was dangerously inexperienced throughout its ranks. Most of the staff had only the vaguest notion of what they should be doing, and precious little idea of how to go about it. When Captain Maurice Buckmaster became F section's information officer in March 1941, he was told that the "general idea" was to obtain information concerning occupied France. He sought clarification from another officer. As Buckmaster later recalled

the conversation, he started by asking what SOE was about.

"Subversive activities," was the answer.

"I've gathered that, sir, but what *kind* of subversive activities?"

"I'm not too clear myself, but I think the idea is to sabotage industrial installations in France."

In spite of everything, SOE did score a few early successes. On the night of May 5, 1941, the first F section agent actually to parachutte into France, Georges Bégué, dropped about 20 miles north of Châteauroux, in the unoccupied zone. Carrying a heavy radio transmitter in his suitcase, he walked to the home of a retired French politician who was a personal friend of F section's second-in-command. When the old Frenchman got over his surprise, he agreed to help, and within days Bégué was able to report back to London the addresses of sympathetic contacts in the area. Three more agents followed almost at once, and in the early hours of June 13 an RAF Whitley bomber, guided by lights set out on the grounds of a château near Limoges, dropped two long metal containers packed with submachine guns, fighting knives, plastic explosive and mines with delayed-action fuses. For the French patriots waiting in the darkness, the shadow war could at last begin in earnest. Those two containers were the first of nearly 100,000 supply packets to thud onto French soil during the German Occupation.

While making the arrangements for the airdrop, Georges

Bégué had an unpleasant foretaste of the dangers in store for all radio operators working with the Resistance. Almost as soon as he began calling London for instructions, the German wireless interception service picked up his Morse transmissions and tried to jam them by transmitting a signal on the same frequency. Vichy police were alerted to look out for strangers around Châteauroux, and direction-finding vans, each one containing a device that could home in on a radio source by means of a special antenna, started cruising the streets to find him. He knew that his freedom depended on keeping transmission time to an absolute minimum.

How could he get information from London without using his transmitter to make radio contact? The solution was simple but brilliant: Enlist the BBC. To cut down the number of transmissions he and his fellow agents would have to make, Bégué suggested that the BBC foreign service should beam messages to underground operatives. This idea was to have far-reaching consequences, leading to an elaborate system of "personal messages" broadcast every evening over the BBC's powerful transmitters to agents and resistance movements throughout Western Europe. Some sounded like simple family greetings ("Jean sends a kiss to Nicole"), some were pointless ("Flora had a red neck") and some were utterly meaningless ("Is Napoleon's hat still at Perros-Guirec?"). But to SOE agents who were aware of their significance, they meant a courier had arrived safely, or a *parachutage* would take place that night, or a railway line should be sabotaged. The Germans expanded endless energy trying to fathom this primitive code, to no avail.

SOE was learning fast from experience, but there was a great deal to learn. The first agents who parachuted into the occupied countries had no reception committees to greet them when they hit the ground. Like Georges Bégué, they carried only the name and address of a stranger who might be willing to help. Often the names of these first contacts were provided by expatriates who had made their way to London when their countries had been overrun. If an SOE agent was lucky, his contact either would be already involved in an embryonic resistance network or would know someone who was. In areas where there were no known sympathizers, the agent was obliged to make cautious inquiries about local resistance. If no resistance group existed in the area, his orders were to attempt to start one. Some-

times an agent was fortunate enough to be dropping into a locale he knew well, where he had friends he could trust. Even in such promising situations, he became a fugitive once he touched the soil of Europe. Unfriendly police and Gestapo spies were everyhere, and a single mistake could lead to capture, torture and death.

The agents who volunteered for this hazardous duty, both men and women, were recruited from all walks of life. The first requirement, of course, was an ability to speak the language of the country concerned. In the Dutch and Scandinavian sections of SOE almost all the recruits were of those nationalities, but in the French and Belgian sections a fair number of agents were bilingual British. Among those recruited during 1941 were bankers, actors, journalists, wine merchants, lawyers, artists, teachers, film directors, dress designers, mothers and housewives.

Mostly they were approached without being told the precise nature of the work involved. If they were thought suitable and willing, they were sent to various homes in southern England, where the furtive craft of the secret agent was explained by instructors who were former agents themselves, many of them veterans of World War I. These introductory lessons were followed by physical toughening at a Commando school in Scotland, plus parachute training, and instruction in unarmed combat, silent killing and wireless operation, and finally by a course at "finishing school," where recruits were put through simulated Gestapo interrogations and left in no doubt as to their slender chances of staying alive if caught.

SOE research scientists kept the training establishments well supplied with ideas and new equipment, ranging from matchsticks hollowed out to hold microfilm to mines disguised as horse droppings. Another SOE enterprise ensured that the agents were properly dressed. At a small factory in the garment-trade area of London, refugees cut and sewed clothes in European styles—sometimes with genuine labels taken from the clothes of foreigners arriving from abroad.

In addition to the technology, training and tailoring, all

Roman Garby-Czerniawski (far left), a former Polish Air Force pilot, helped to organize a spy ring known as Interallié and audaciously set up a clandestine radio in a Paris apartment (circled, left) not far from the Gestapo headquarters. On May 10, 1941, his group transmitted a coded message to London—the first radio contact with France in a year.

To supply Resistance groups with small arms, explosives, medicine and clothing, SOE employed this metal supply canister, which was nearly six feet long and weighed approximately 100 pounds when fully loaded.

THE MOON SQUADRON'S RESOURCEFUL AIR SHUTTLE

Produced in a number of specialized models, the versatile Lysander was used by the British not only for clandestine transport but also for low-level strafing attacks, artillery reconnaissance and air-sea rescue missions.

On the night of October 19, 1940, RAF pilot W. J. Farley swooped down onto a moonlit field near Montigny in occupied France, picked up Philip Schneidau, a British agent, then swiftly took off. A single shot from below smashed Farley's compass, and when heavy clouds blotted out landmarks, he wandered far off course. He finally crash-landed in Scotland—with no lasting damage to himself or his passenger.

Farley's harrowing mission was the first of more than 180 successful secret RAF landings in France alone, in which more than 800 persons were either dropped off or flown back to Britain. His outfit, known as the "Moon Squadron," generally flew light, single-engined Lysanders similar to the one above; the plane's rugged undercarriage and ability to land and take off in

only 400 yards opened up much of the European countryside to surreptitious visits. Stripped of armament and fitted with an extra fuel tank, the "Lizzy" had a range of 400 to 450 miles.

The squadron flew as many missions as weather permitted during the week before and after each full moon. Between these "moon periods," the fliers spent their days helping to train agents who would be delivered to the occupied countries to organize resistance groups. At least one phase of the tutelage was very much in the pilots' own interest: they taught the recruits to find suitable landing strips—free of ruts or soft mud—and to mark them with flares.

Regrettably, not every student learned well. John Nesbitt-Dufort *(right)* returned from his first mission to France with tele-

phone wires wrapped around the undercarriage of his Lysander—the consequence of an ill-planned airstrip. Nesbitt-Dufort, who eventually rose to squadron leadership, suffered more than his share of bad luck. On another flight, the wings of his Lysander began to ice over after a pickup, and he was forced to land again in France. A hidden ditch disabled the plane *(right)*, but he managed to evade local security police and return to England by moonlight shuttle a month later.

Despite the perilous nature of the job, the squadron lost only 13 Lysanders and six pilots in four years of operation—a small price to pay for same-day transport service that did much to maintain the bonds between intelligence headquarters and the agents working in the field.

A Sussex cottage dating to the 17th Century served as the Moon Squadron's headquarters.

Squadron Leader
Nesbitt-Dufort

Forced down by icing, Nesbitt-Dufort's Lysander comes to rest in a ditch.

agents needed an ample measure of luck to survive in the summer of 1941, and at that time good luck was in short supply. Gilbert Turck, a Paris architect who had escaped to England soon after the defeat of France, had more than his fair share of troubles when he dropped back into France, near Montluçon, on the night of August 6, with SOE instructions to organize arms dumps. "Sitting in the plane waiting to jump, I was not afraid; I simply did not think about being afraid," Turck recalled. "I had an extraordinary feeling that my whole life was a preparation for that moment. My parents had instilled in me a great sense of duty and devotion to France and it seemed to me to be perfectly natural to do what I was doing. So when the signal came to jump, I pushed myself out of the plane with such vigor and enthusiasm that I hit the underside of the wing, knocked myself out, and dropped to the ground completely unconscious.

"When I came to, I was in a police station, surrounded by policemen. Apparently two peasants had found me lying on the ground and had taken me there. I was groggy for a couple of days and can't remember very clearly what happened, but I know I was taken to a military prison in Clermont-Ferrand for interrogation."

To his own amazement, Turck managed to secure his release by spinning a story about bribing the RAF to drop him back into France because he hated the English so much he could not tolerate the thought of staying there. Once out of prison, he moved down to Marseilles, following instructions, and set about organizing arms dumps. He also rented a spacious home, the Villa des Bois, which he intended to utilize as a "safe house" for fellow agents.

More agents followed Turck into Vichy France within a matter of weeks. One arrived at night in a Lysander, a light, single-engined aircraft whose ability to land or take off in a distance of only 200 yards enabled it to use meadows and fields with ease. Ten agents parachuted in, and four landed near Perpignan from H.M.S. *Fidelity*, a Royal Navy ship based at Gibraltar.

They had little in common, these men, except perhaps the knowledge that there was a safe house in Marseilles called the Villa des Bois. What they did not know was that the Vichy police also knew.

The cover of the Villa des Bois had been blown early in the game when one of the newly arrived SOE agents was arrested with the address of the safe house in his pocket. An unsuspecting Turck left Marseilles for Paris early in September to visit his fiancée. While he was away, Vichy policemen transformed his house into a *souricière*—a mousetrap—to catch visiting agents. They installed a man who resembled Turck, and then they waited.

One by one, SOE agents rang the bell at the Villa des Bois, were invited inside, and were immediately arrested. The last visitor, appearing at the door on October 24, was SOE's pioneering Georges Bégué, the sole remaining radio operator in the unoccupied zone. His arrest left the few F-section agents still free in Vichy France completely cut off from communication with London. To compound the disaster, Gestapo direction-finding teams were closing in on André Bloch, the only SOE radio operator working in the occupied zone, at Le Mans, 115 miles southwest of Paris. He transmitted his last message on November 12, and London never heard from him again.

Turck learned of the string of arrests from friends in Lyons when he was on his way back to Marseilles; thus he avoided walking into the mousetrap. But by then he was a marked man, and in July of 1942, when he was again in Paris, his resistance career came to an abrupt and somewhat ignominious end. "I had been meeting with other resistants in the back room of a small shop called France Parfums on the Boulevard St. Germain and I stopped at a *pissoir* on my way home. When I looked up I suddenly saw three men in civilian clothes, with guns drawn, advancing toward me from different directions. There was no possibility of escape from that situation; I was handcuffed and taken away."

It was the beginning of an endless ordeal for Turck. "The questioning was very thorough and went on for a long time," he later recalled, "but I did not give them any information. My main worry at the time was that my fiancée would be compromised. I had borrowed her bicycle permit and, seeing that, they went off to search her apartment, where I had stacked a lot of explosives in an old armchair on one of the landings on the staircase. I learned later that they turned the apartment over, but never took a second glance at the armchair on the stairs." Turck was eventually sent to Buchenwald—but he survived.

On Baker Street, the SOE chiefs despaired over the omi-

nous silence from France. They had no way of telling how, where or why their wireless operators had been captured. Neither did they know how many other agents had fallen into the hands of the enemy, and they began to wonder if *any* of their men in France were still free, or even alive.

At last, a coded message came through from Paris on New Year's Day, 1942, and jubilation replaced the gloom on Baker Street. The sender identified himself as Pierre de Vomécourt, one of three brothers who had been organizing resistance activity since May 1941. After briefly explaining the events of the past few months, the message concluded with an urgent request that more money be dispatched to those agents still operative.

The signal contained prearranged codes to prove its authenticity, and de Vomécourt was in fact the author of the message—but he was not the sender. It had been broadcast by the Abwehr, the German military intelligence.

De Vomécourt had no idea of what was afoot. He did not possess a radio himself and had spent weeks searching for a way to reestablish contact with London. Eventually, a lawyer friend introduced him to Mathilde Carré, an attractive Frenchwoman in her early thirties who was known to her friends as Lily and to her resistance compatriots as "La Chatte" (The Cat). She and de Vomécourt met in the Café Georges V on the Champs-Elysées on December 26, 1941. La Chatte explained that she had been working with a Polish intelligence circuit that had been broken up by the Germans. She had escaped arrest, as had the circuit's radio operator, who was still in contact with London. She said she would gladly send a message to SOE for de Vomécourt.

Sitting alone at another table in the café was a man in civilian clothes whose round, horn-rimmed spectacles gave him a slightly owlish appearance. He pretended to take no notice of the quiet but urgent conversation between La Chatte and de Vomécourt. He was Sergeant Hugo Bleicher of the Abwehr. La Chatte was his paramour.

La Chatte's story was true in some respects. She had indeed been a trusted member of Interallié, a Polish intelligence circuit in contact with British military intelligence. But she neglected to tell de Vomécourt that when the circuit was penetrated by the Abwehr, she, too, had been arrested. Her interrogation had been conducted by Bleicher over a sumptuous meal in a private suite at the Hôtel

Edouard VII, on the Avenue de l'Opéra, which the Abwehr had commandeered as its Paris headquarters. By the following morning, La Chatte had agreed to turn double agent.

During the next few days, La Chatte led Bleicher to the homes and meeting places of the members of Interallié who were still free. She calmly identified one of them, a former lover named Claude Jouffret, by greeting him with a kiss at the Café Louis XIV. Abwehr agents seized Interallié's four radio transmitters and moved them to a house in the Paris suburb of Saint-Germain-en-Laye, where contact with London was resumed. La Chatte knew all the codes, schedules for transmission and prearranged security checks, so London had no reason to suspect anything was wrong.

Unfortunately for the enterprising Sergeant Bleicher and his hopes of subverting SOE's French network, de Vomécourt was soon seized by undefinable suspicions of La Chatte's sincerity. At the end of January he tried a simple test, asking La Chatte if she could get hold of some forged identity documents. She showed up the following day with a perfect set of papers, complete with German stamps. Her efficiency was too good to be true. On top of this disturbing feat, she produced a photograph and, with studied casualness, asked de Vomécourt if he recognized the man. It was Michael Trotobas, another SOE agent.

De Vomécourt immediately accused La Chatte of working for the Germans. She broke down in tears and confessed. According to the rules of the game, de Vomécourt should have killed her on the spot, warned his companions to disband and then fled himself. But he had formulated other plans. The woman had turned once, he reasoned, and she might well turn again. Pierre de Vomécourt persuaded La Chatte to become a triple agent.

Bleicher, blissfully unaware of the fact that the treacherous La Chatte was again working for the Allies, was soon being fed wonderful new intelligence by his faithless lover. She told him that de Vomécourt was planning to organize a meeting in Paris of all the major resistance leaders to coordinate their future activity. At this very moment, she said, he was making arrangements to leave for England to brief a senior general, who would return with him in time for the conference. Would it not be a good idea if she could persuade de Vomécourt to take her along? Think of the information she could supply when she returned! Bleicher

thought it would be a very good idea indeed and, after some difficulty, managed to convince his superiors.

So it was that the Abwehr obligingly arranged through the Interallié transmitters for a Royal Navy motor torpedo boat to pick up an SOE agent and a triple agent from a remote cove on the Breton coast.

The whole bizarre episode was suitably punctuated by slapstick confusion. At midnight on February 12, 1942, with Abwehr officers watching from behind bushes, a dinghy rowed ashore from a British MTB waiting just outside the cove. As La Chatte tried to get on board, the dinghy overturned and threw her into the sea. De Vomécourt dragged her back onto the beach, where she stood dripping and furious while the dinghy crew struggled to right their craft. But the sea got rougher and the pickup had to be abandoned. A week later, another attempt was made. This time there was a muddle over the point of rendezvous, and the MTB waited off one cove while de Vomécourt and La Chatte fruitlessly signaled from another.

At last, on the moonlit night of February 26, they embarked for London. A comfortable flat, wired with hidden microphones, had been provided for La Chatte, and she spent several months happily talking her head off to sympathetic British intelligence officers. When she had no more to say, she was removed, protesting violently, to an English prison, where she stayed for the rest of the War.

Pierre de Vomécourt parachuted back into France on April 1 to resume his resistance activities. But Bleicher, spurred by ruffled pride, picked up his trail and arrested him in Paris on April 25. De Vomécourt was beaten mercilessly during interrogation at Fresnes prison; most of his front

Mathilde Carré, the infamous triple agent known to Germans and Allies alike as "La Chatte" (The Cat), listens impassively at her trial for high treason, held in France in 1949. She was sentenced to death for helping the Germans break up the Interallié spy ring in 1942. But the sentence later was commuted to life imprisonment, and La Chatte was pardoned in 1954.

teeth were knocked out. But he remained stubbornly silent.

After the capture of de Vomécourt, his circuit was wiped out and F section of SOE was left, temporarily, without a single organized network in occupied France. But French agents, reporting directly to de Gaulle's intelligence organization in London, the Bureau Central de Renseignements et d'Action (BCRA), were faring somewhat better—and soon would pull off an astounding intelligence coup that dramatically affected the outcome of the War.

At the beginning of May, René Duchez, a house painter in the Normandy city of Caen, was hired to refurbish the local offices of Organization Todt, Germany's public-works bureau, which was building Hitler's Atlantic Wall—the defenses against the anticipated Allied invasion—along the whole west coast of occupied Europe. Duchez was 40 years old, a nondescript little man with a small mustache, a taste for the local apple brandy and a smile so persistent that some acquaintances thought him simple-minded. Duchez was also a member of a resistance network: the Confrérie Notre-Dame, set up by a BCRA agent, Gilbert Renault.

Duchez seemed so patently harmless that when he arrived with his wallpaper samples and pots and brushes at Organization Todt, the Germans took very little notice of him. He was briefly left alone in an office with a pile of maps on the desk. Quickly Duchez grabbed the top map and stuck it behind a heavy, gilt-framed mirror on the wall. Five days later, when he had finished the job, he walked out with his prize hidden in the bottom of an old paint tin in which he carried his brushes.

The map, 10 feet long and 2 feet wide, was a top-secret blueprint of part of the Atlantic Wall. It was passed along to Gilbert Renault, who soon thereafter received a warning from the resistance grapevine that the Gestapo was closing in on him. Renault decided to flee to England with his wife, three young children and the invaluable blueprint. He made arrangements for a fishing boat to smuggle him to mid-Channel, where a British trawler would pick him up.

On the evening of June 16, Renault had a farewell dinner with friends at an inn in the coastal village of Pont-Aven. He left a biscuit tin containing the map and two parcels of equally incriminating intelligence dispatches on a bench at the entrance, just as if they were unimportant, store-bought packages. "I took care to sit so that I had them under continual observation," he later reported to the Free French in London. "We had just begun our dinner when half a dozen German submarine officers came clattering in. They put their caps down on my boxes. After that I knew I need not worry—no one would touch them."

When the meal was over, Renault retrieved his packages, and the next morning he and his family jammed themselves into the smelly, coffin-sized gear lockers of the fishing boat. The captain and crew of the tiny vessel knew that they might not make it out of the harbor; all boats had to line up for possible inspection before departure, although the Germans usually eased their own task by making spot checks rather than searching every vessel.

Renault was squeezed into the forward locker, desperately feeding chocolate drops to his restless 18-month-old baby, Michael, when the boat approached the German checkpoint on a jetty at the harbor entrance. He felt the engine die, and then heard German voices and the sound of their boots on the stone of the jetty. Miraculously, the baby remained silent. Agonizing minutes later, the engine came to life again and soon the boat was pitching heavily in the swells of the Channel. As it happened, the French vessel just in front of the Renaults' craft had been turned inside out, but theirs had merely been glanced at and waved on.

The map soon lay unfolded in the offices of the British intelligence chiefs. They were stunned by the importance of the document, which revealed all the planned German coastal defenses along the entire coast of Normandy from Cherbourg almost to Le Havre—the strong points and the weak ones. Thus René Duchez, the house painter from Caen, and Gilbert Renault, the resistance chief, were instrumental in helping the Allies plan for their invasion on D-Day in June 1944.

The Germans, of course, were vitally interested in the time and place of the Allied invasion they expected. And German intelligence could reasonably speculate in 1942 that this crucial information would come from a most unlikely source—SOE itself. Logic suggested that SOE would forewarn all its field agents in Western Europe of the impending invasion. If this turned out to be the case, the Abwehr was bound to share the secret, for every SOE agent in Holland was in their hands—although London did not know it.

The German intelligence coup in Holland began unfolding in the winter of 1941-1942. Agents of the Abwehr knew that somewhere in the Dutch capital, The Hague, a clandestine radio operator was in contact with London. They also knew, through interceptions, that the Morse call sign used to identify his station was RLS, and that he transmitted every Friday evening at 6:30. By Friday evening, March 6, their direction-finding radio teams had zeroed in on the source of his signal.

It was cold that day, and Hubert Lauwers, the SOE operator, sat in his overcoat in the parlor of a friend's small apartment on Fahrenheitstraat, waiting for 6:30 p.m. The curtains were drawn across the window so that the glow from the tubes of Lauwers' radio set could not be seen from the street. Close by the set were several messages, coded in the cipher he had been taught during his training in Britain the year before.

As the hands of his wrist watch crawled to the appointed time, he slipped on a pair of headphones and carefully began tapping out his call sign. Almost immediately, the door behind him burst open and the young Dutch friend who lived in the apartment entered the room. There were suspicious-looking cars at the end of the street, he said. It might be trouble.

Lauwers switched off the set, crossed to the window and peered out through a slit in the curtains. The cars were there, all right, but so far the street had not been blocked.

Lauwers concluded that the Germans' direction-finding equipment had not quite pinpointed the apartment and that escape was still possible. The transmitter was swiftly packed into its black attaché case and dropped out of a rear window. Lauwers then stuffed the messages into his pocket and, with his friend, hurried down the stairs. At the front door they paused to compose themselves before stepping out into the street.

Apparently deep in conversation, the two men strolled down Fahrenheitstraat away from the cars. Nothing happened. Not until they reached the junction with Cypressestraat did Lauwers dare to risk a glance backward. Still nothing. They turned into Cypressestraat and quickened their pace, believing themselves out of danger. Suddenly there was a squeal of brakes as they were overtaken by two large cars. A third car mounted the sidewalk in front of them, and about a dozen men, waving revolvers, jumped out and surrounded them.

Lauwers was thrust against a wall and searched. His ciphered messages were found at once and flourished triumphantly under his nose; the game was indisputably up. Lauwers was taken back to the apartment on Fahrenheitstraat, where his jettisoned transmitter had already been discovered, undamaged, neatly straddling two lines of washing at the rear of the building.

"On my arrival," Lauwers recalled later, "I found several Germans examining my transmitter and others sniffing round the room in a search for suspicious material. I knew that their efforts would be in vain, as there was nothing more to be discovered. I could not restrain a broad grin when an undersized police official showed a secret paper with great solemnity to his chief and threw me a triumphant look at the same time." The agent knew that the paper was worthless—a simple mathematical formula torn from the notebook of his friend, who was a part-time engineering student. The little policeman, said Lauwers, "looked angry and disappointed when a look of surprise and a scarcely discernible smile crossed his superior's face. Extraordinary, but this German clearly had a sense of humor!"

The German with a sense of humor was Major Hermann

The two French patriots who made off with blueprints of Hitler's Atlantic Wall went on to win more resistance laurels. House painter René Duchez (far left), who stole the plans from a German office in Caen in 1942, continued to pass on to the Allies detailed information about the Normandy area right up to the eve of the invasion. Gilbert Renault, wearing a beret in the photograph at left, later rose through the ranks to become a colonel and a member of the nationwide resistance coordinating committee. The photograph was taken on the trawler that smuggled him out of France with the Normandy plans (and his wife and infant son).

Giskes, commander of section 111F, the military counter-espionage department of the Abwehr in the Netherlands. Giskes, aged 46, was an intelligent, dedicated officer with great charm and sensitivity. These qualities were to serve him well in bringing off the coup that was eventually regarded as SOE's worst defeat.

It had long been an Abwehr ambition to "play back" a captured radio transmitter, an operation the Germans referred to as *Englandspiel*—the game against England. This game carried high stakes. If the Germans could conceal from London their capture of a radio operator, and could keep the radio link open, they might be able to penetrate the heart of the enemy intelligence service. They could pass misleading information to London, and receive in return the details of their enemy's organizations and intentions.

But London had taken precautions against this technique. Every radio operator had his own security check—a mistake or a word he included in every transmission. The absence of a security check would indicate to London that the operator was in trouble.

Plainly, the easiest way to surmount this obstacle was to get a captured radio operator to turn double agent. Giskes set out to persuade the young Dutchman to cooperate. There followed, during Lauwers' interrogtation at Scheveningen prison on the outskirts of The Hague, a curious psychological battle between the two men, with each of them playing a role to confound the other.

Giskes was sympathetic and friendly, the very antithesis of the brutal interrogator that Lauwers had been led to expect. "It was important," Giskes later said, "not to treat the prisoner with the severity, hostility and crude methods that were the nightmare of such agents if caught by the Germans, but a friendly understanding should be shown of his proved operational ability, and human sympathy for his misfortune. After a few introductory inquiries touching his health and living conditions, I put to him forcefully that he alone could assist me in my plan to save him. I used every kind of appeal to his intelligence and emphasized how pointless it was for him to throw his life away. He must at least help me to produce one single argument that would enable me to avert the death sentence. To do this he would

simply have to transmit at noon the messages he had been unable to pass when he had been arrested."

Lauwers was not stupid: he knew that Giskes was trying to "turn him around." He had been told at the SOE security school in England that this was likely to happen if he were caught. He had also been told that while he might feel honor bound to refuse to operate his set for the Germans, such conduct would be unwise. The Gestapo had the means to break the strongest man. Far better to play for time by agreeing to work the set. There was no danger, after all, as long as the security check was omitted. It might even give London a chance to play back the set to the Germans.

With an appropriate show of reluctance, Lauwers finally agreed to cooperate; he would simply botch his security check, which was based on the first two figures of his agent number—1672. According to instructions from London, he was supposed to make a mistake in every 16th letter in the text of his transmissions. By not making these mistakes, he would alert London to his capture.

But the Germans were experienced enough to know that SOE radio operators had secret security checks, and they were anxious that Lauwers include his so that London would think nothing was wrong. For his captors, Lauwers concocted a lie. He told them that his security check was to change "stop," a word that appeared frequently in transmissions, to "stip" or "step" in every message. Giskes was delighted that his poor prisoner was proving so helpful.

After missing only two scheduled transmissions, Lauwers reopened contact with London—but this time from a German radio interception station at Scheveningen. A German radio operator listened in with his hand on the key of a jamming transmitter, in case Lauwers tried to depart from the text. Lauwers did not, of course, because he was certain that London would spot the absence of his real security checks and realize that he was in German hands.

Unfortunately for SOE, things went disastrously wrong. London not only failed to notice that agent 1672 had omitted his security checks but three days later sent Lauwers instructions to prepare for the reception of another agent who was to be dropped during the next full-moon period.

In the early hours of March 28, 1942, a Dutch agent with

the code name "Abor" jumped from an aircraft circling over the lights that a reception committee had laid out on a remote moorland in northern Holland. He was greeted in the dark by a Dutch voice whispering the appropriate code word. The reception committee helped him bury his parachute, relieved him of his revolver—in case, he said, they were stopped by a German patrol—then led him to a car where Major Giskes was waiting. Abor thought it was some bizarre joke when handcuffs were slipped over his wrists.

Within the next few weeks, with the help of names and addresses deftly cadged from an unsuspecting London, the Germans arrested nine agents already working in Holland and a number of Dutch Resistance leaders. On the night of May 29, two more agents were dropped straight into the arms of the Gestapo. Another four followed a month later, two the month after that. So it continued, with almost monotonous regularity.

Lauwers, horrified at what was happening, tried three times to warn London by transmitting the word "caught." There was no reaction. By then Giskes was playing back at least four transmitters—and each time a new operator arrived, the Germans could establish another radio link.

The more transmitters being played back, the more complicated the deception became. But Giskes maintained the whole elaborate charade with a sure touch. When London ordered the destruction of a radar station about 40 miles southeast of Amsterdam, Giskes staged a mock attack so that local Resistance groups would confirm that an assault had taken place. Then a radio operator reported back to London that the effort had failed and that some casualties had been sustained. When London ordered sabotage in Rotterdam, Giskes had a canal barge carrying scrap metal blown up. The explosion damaged nothing of value, but news of it convinced London that its Dutch agents were on the job. When London ordered the assassination of leading Dutch Nazis, Giskes hedged and complained that the task was impossible without a rifle with telescopic sights.

Even London's insistence that an agent should be sent back to report progress in person did not stop the resourceful Major Giskes. He first complained that the agent suggested was too important to be spared, then raised bothersome questions about how he would make the trip to England and back. London thereupon provided a contact address in Brussels for an escape line that would pass their man back. The Germans penetrated the escape line, arrested as many people as they could find, then reported to London that unfortunately the agent had been killed in a traffic accident in the south of France.

The deception could not, of course, go on forever, although it must have appeared to the Germans that there was no end to the gullibility of their opposite numbers in Britain. In August 1943, two agents escaped from a Dutch prison and made their way back to England with news of what had been happening in Holland. Even then, some SOE chiefs refused to believe their story, because Giskes had sent a message to London warning that the two men had been caught by the Gestapo and "turned around."

Before *Englandspiel* finally ended, the Germans had captured no fewer than 52 Allied agents, all but one from SOE. More than 4,000 messages had been exchanged with London, and the information received had directly contributed to a further 350 arrests. In addition, British airdrops supplied the Germans with 570 containers and 150 parcels containing 15,200 kilograms of explosive, 8,000 small arms, 300 machine guns, 2,000 hand grenades, 75 radio transmitters, 500,000 rounds of ammunition, 40 bicycles and large quantities of such items as clothing, tobacco, tinned food, coffee and chocolate.

Major Giskes formally ended the episode with a final, exquisitely sarcastic message sent to London on April 1, 1944—All Fools' Day—over the 10 transmitters still in operation. "We understand that you have been endeavoring for some time to do business in Holland without our assistance," the message read. "We regret this the more since we have acted for so long as your sole representatives in this country, to our mutual satisfaction. Nevertheless we can assure you that, should you be thinking of paying us a visit on the Continent on any extensive scale, we shall give your emissaries the same attention as we have hitherto, and a similarly warm welcome. Hoping to see you."

The postscript to the story was less amusing. Forty-six of the 52 captured agents were eventually executed.

THE LONDON CONNECTION

An SOE agent, elaborately disguised as a nanny, steadies his revolver on a baby carriage during a mock ambush at a secret training installation in Britain.

CLEARING HOUSE FOR SUBVERSION

Between July 1943 and February 1944, an audacious quartet of British-trained secret agents spread a trail of death and destruction through southeastern France. The men—a former student, a taxi-business manager, a mechanic's helper and a fireman—assassinated a dozen Gestapo officers in Lyons, blew up a German cannon factory in nearby Le Creusot and stopped the shipment of German war supplies through France's inland waterways by sabotaging vital canal locks.

This deadly little outfit was one of scores of teams dispatched from London by the Special Operations Executive (SOE), founded in 1940 with orders to "coordinate all action, by way of sabotage and subversion, against the enemy overseas." SOE operations grew into a massive campaign of destruction and harassment throughout occupied Europe. In 1943 these activities were placed in the hands of veteran SOE leader Major-General Colin McVean Gubbins, who had come to appreciate guerrilla tactics the hard way—by fighting against rebel bands in Ireland in the 1920s.

By 1944, Gubbins' unorthodox organization had attracted some 13,000 daring volunteers, including about 3,000 women. Some were members of Britain's officer corps, but most agents were foreigners with close knowledge of the language and customs of the country in which they would operate. Of these, a number were married couples; SOE, fearing that the concern of spouses for each other would impair their judgment, gave them separate assignments.

After varied and intensive training, SOE's agents were smuggled into Europe by plane, parachute, boat, even by submarine. There they made contact with local Resistance groups and took on the Germans with the weapons and explosives SOE sent in after them. With each delivery of explosives, SOE sent an instruction manual written by Gubbins himself and translated into 14 European languages. The pamphlet, "How to Use High Explosives," was by far the most popular work in the annals of subversive literature: Hundreds of thousands of copies circulated in the underground, teaching the dark arts of sabotage that would do so much to cripple the German war machine.

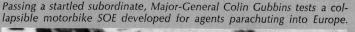
Passing a startled subordinate, Major-General Colin Gubbins tests a collapsible motorbike SOE developed for agents parachuting into Europe.

Stately Beaulieu Manor, near Southampton, housed the training staff of several nearby SOE schools where agents learned the skills of clandestine warfare.

In a London radio studio, announcers for the BBC's French-language service read news bulletins—and coded SOE instructions meant for agents in the field.

Sliding down a makeshift rope bridge by means of a simple harness, an SOE agent-in-training crosses a river as a smoke grenade explodes beneath him. Other

A CURRICULUM OF DEADLY SKILLS

The training program for potential agents began with paramilitary courses conducted in country houses in southern England. Promising recruits were then routed to a much more difficult school in the remote Scottish highlands. There, they learned to live off the meager offerings of the land, including the wild turnips that inspired a wry nickname for the survival lessons—"the turnip course."

The next course in the SOE curriculum was parachute training at a jump school near Manchester, followed by specialized training of various sorts at secluded mansions scattered around the English countryside. At a house in Hertfordshire, two veterans of the Shanghai police taught the fine points of hand-to-hand combat; other houses offered lessons in the use of small arms, in radio operation and in sabotage

In a practice ambush, SOE men interrogate one of their instructors, disguised as a German courier.

conditioning included grueling forced marches.

Preparing agents for missions, SOE tailors fashion garments in the styles of the occupied countries.

techniques. After completing their formal training, the fledgling agents were given their first assignments—along with false identities and instructions on locating safe houses and setting up courier systems. On departing, they also received an L-pill—a lethal capsule to swallow when faced with capture and torture too terrible to bear.

With his binoculars in hand, Captain Daniel Lomenech (left) stands on the deck of his trawler (above). Captain Lomenech and his boat frequently ferried SOE agents and supplies to Brittany from the south coast of England.

FELUCCA FERRIES AND THE "SHETLAND BUS"

One of the trickiest tasks facing SOE was to land agents and cargo on the heavily patrolled coasts of occupied Europe. SOE relied primarily on fleets of weather-beaten fishing boats made available by owners who had fled their homelands when the Germans arrived.

In the early years of the Occupation, the most colorful of these maritime shuttles consisted of two feluccas, small, slow sardine boats, which sailed between Gibraltar and the Mediterranean coast of France. Manned by devil-may-care crews of Polish seamen, the feluccas delivered SOE agents and small quantities of arms until the German occupation of Vichy France in 1942 made continued landings too risky.

But the most successful seaborne supply service of SOE was the "Shetland Bus," which linked Britain's Shetland Islands and the fjords of Norway. The rugged Norwegian fishing boats braved fierce storms and bristling German defenses on three-week journeys that had to be made in the dead of winter, under cover of the long subarctic nights. The dauntless Norwegians made a total of 207 round trips, putting ashore 219 agents and delivering 314 tons of arms, explosives and communications gear.

Bound for occupied Norway, SOE agents and crewmen gather on the deck of the Norwegian fishing vessel Arthur as it prepares to leave the port of Lunna in the Shetland Islands.

Two men struggle to lower a fish crate filled with weapons and ammunition into a ship's cargo hold. The boat was to rendezvous with agents in Denmark.

Four Danish resistants eagerly unpack a supply container that has been parachuted to them by SOE.

A CROSS-CHANNEL SUPPLY SERVICE

Through the services of the RAF, SOE air-dropped tens of thousands of tons of war matériel to Resistance networks in occupied Europe. The supply missions—flown mainly by bombers—demanded pinpoint navigation and split-second timing; most of the flights had to be made at night.

At first, the results were disappointing; enemy flak, bad weather and the inexperience of pilots and agents forced the scrubbing of 55 per cent of the flights. But by 1944, the failure rate had been cut almost in half by the improvement of procedures and the introduction of new ground-to-air communications gear.

Following arrangements made by radio, a nighttime reception committee of several resistants would gather at a rendezvous point, usually an open field several miles from the nearest town or German outpost. The drop zone was not marked out until the last minute: When airplane engines were heard, three men with bicycle lamps or flashlights deployed in a row, while the leader positioned himself off to the side and signaled with his light in Morse code to indicate to the plane that all appeared to be safe. The crewmen then released parachute-equipped supply canisters.

Thousands of these nocturnal rendezvous occurred, supplying the Resistance networks and their SOE agents with the tools needed for their underground war. In France alone, SOE air-dropped more than 650 tons of explosives, 723,000 hand grenades and some half-million small arms, including 198,000 Sten guns, 128,000 rifles, 20,000 Bren guns and 58,000 pistols.

Photographed at the instant of impact, a caniste

A twin-engined Hudson bomber flies a mission for SOE. In addition to making occasional supply drops, Hudsons were used to pick up and deliver SOE's French agents.

filled with supplies for a Resistance network lands in a field in France. SOE air-dropped more than 10,000 tons of supplies into France during the Occupation.

SUBVERSIVE GADGETRY

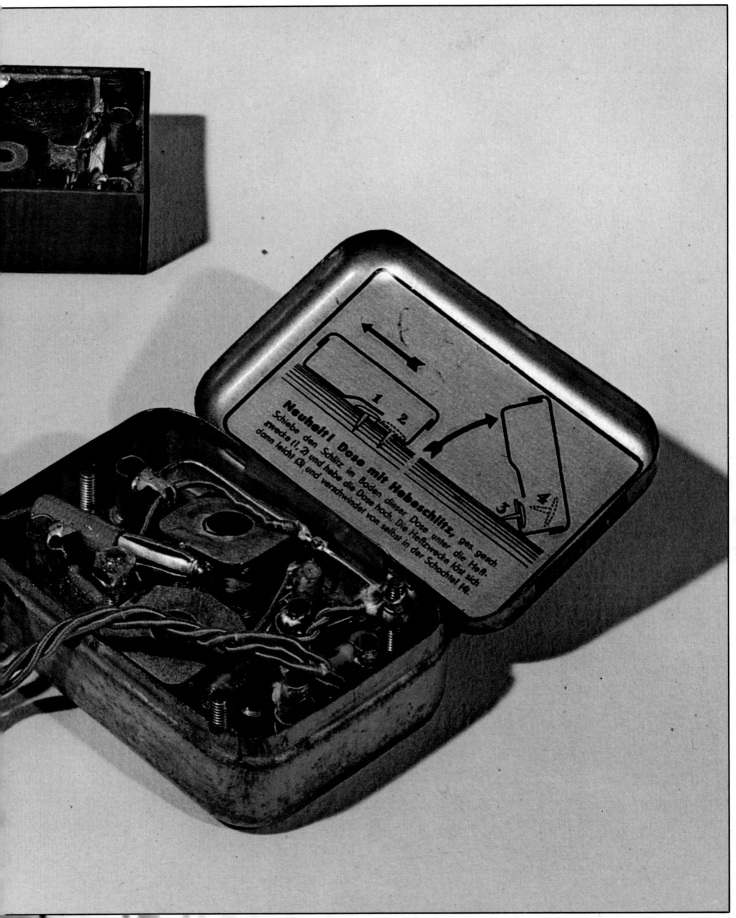

Neuheit! Dose mit Hebeschlitz, ges. gesch
Schiebe den Schlitz im Boden dieser Dose unter die Heftzwecke (1, 2) und hebe die Dose hoch. Die Heftzwecke löst sich
dann leicht (3) und verschwindet von selbst in der Schachtel (4).

TOOLS OF A DANGEROUS TRADE

Preparing an incendiary bomb, a resistant in Holland carefully pours flammable material into an empty can of VIM, a popular Dutch cleanser.

In the autumn of 1943, Gustave Bieler, an SOE agent operating near Saint-Quentin, France, handed out cans filled with a secret substance to several railway men who he knew were friendly to the cause. The tins contained what appeared to be ordinary lubricating grease; actually, it was an abrasive compound that quickly wore out any parts to which it was applied. Before long, Bieler's efficient saboteurs had put 10 locomotives out of action with the help of the diabolical goo.

A vast array of no less remarkable equipment and weapons was employed by secret agents and resistants throughout occupied Europe. Of the outstanding examples shown on these pages, some were fashioned by ingenious individuals who were working secretly in private homes and shops in the occupied countries. These amateur artisans built everything from crystal radio sets to deadly pistols, booby traps, time bombs and grenades.

The other main sources of secret equipment were the laboratories and research sections of SOE, the OSS and various military intelligence departments. Their most important products were radios used by the underground to exchange Morse-code messages with headquarters or with other operators in the field. SOE technicians led the way in developing compact, lightweight receiver-transmitters, and the advanced model called the A Mark III *(right)* was issued to agents by the hundreds.

Allied scientists also focused their inventive efforts on improving microfilm techniques and on creating a host of extraordinary implements of death and destruction. Weapon designers secreted guns in pens and tire pumps, and demolition experts disguised explosives as loaves of bread that blew up when sliced, or as lumps of coal that detonated when shoveled into boilers. The never-ending parade of innocent-looking yet deadly devices succeeded in fostering uncertainty and fear among German troops and Occupation administrators. According to one SOE agent, the Germans "wondered what articles of everyday use, if any, were safe to touch."

Innocuous-seeming leather cases (inset, top) held two short-wave transceivers used by Allied agents. The reddish-brown valise housed SOE's 30-pound Type 3 Mark II (above), while the black case housed the 11-inch-long Type A Mark III, whose powerful signal carried more than 600 miles. Both of the transceivers could operate on either electric current or batteries like the one concealed in the wicker-covered carboy at right.

A record player (top) was transformed into a wo-tube radio receiver (bottom) when the urntable was moved and a headset attached.

Mundane objects (top)—a business directory, an iron and a sofa leg—hid tiny receivers (bottom)

camera and a vacuum bottle housed radios. An anti-Hitler German soldier provided the maker of the bottled set with stolen spare parts

INGENIOUS WAYS OF KEEPING INFORMED

With the press censored and home radios often confiscated by the Occupation authorities, citizens who were eager to learn the war news constructed their own radio receivers and tuned them to the powerful transmitters of the BBC. Since possession of a radio was an offense punishable by fines and imprisonment, a large part of the makers' ingenuity was devoted to camouflage and concealment.

Alv Bjerkelo, a gifted handyman in Sandnessjoen, Norway, turned out a number of cleverly disguised radios, some of them built into vacuum bottles *(left, below)* and sofa legs *(left)*. Another Norwegian radio builder, Thorleif Thorgersen of Stavanger, hid his two-tube receiver in a birdhouse that hung on an outside wall *(right, top)*. A Dutch resistant recalled, "We often buried our homemade radios under coal piles in the basement, or out in the fields under manure piles."

Perhaps the most remarkable concealment of all was fashioned by a Norwegian soldier and dental technician named Arthur Bergfjord. Imprisoned by the Germans in a camp near Breslau, in Poland, Bergfjord built a radio into a fellow inmate's denture plate *(right, center)*. To use the receiver, the inmate removed the denture from his mouth and hooked it up to a battery and headset that had been smuggled into the camp. The twice-false teeth worked remarkably well. Said Bergfjord, "We could hear BBC's European service programs loud and clear."

A birdhouse that actually concealed a primitive receiver never aroused the Germans' suspicions

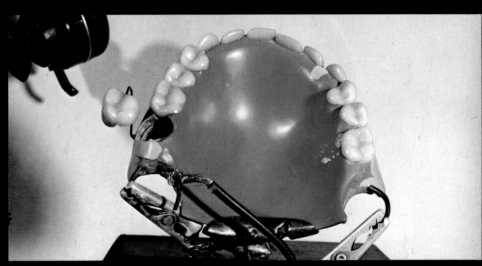

An intricately wired denture plate was able to receive broadcasts from London, 1,200 miles away

An empty Norwegian varnish can proved a perfect hiding place for a radio and headphones

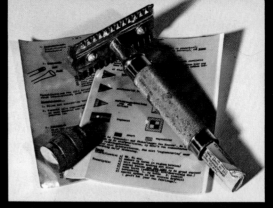
The hollow handle of a safety razor hid printed matter.

A bogus pen concealed messages or a vial of poison (above, right).   *A seemingly ordinary log (top) contained underground newspapers (bottom).*

This beer crate had a secret compartment.

The water tap *(left)* in a lavatory on a Norway-to-Sweden train had a removable cap nut *(top)* in which resistants placed microdot messages. Swedish agents retrieved the dots and transmitted them to England.

Incriminating items were smuggled inside hollow boot heels, altered cans of fish roe, dummy batteries *(bottom)* and home-baked loaves of bread

A NOOK FOR EVERY SECRET NEED

To convey encoded messages and other compromising material, resourceful resistants devised hiding places out of objects ranging from toothpaste tubes to canned goods. Underground workers made use of hollowed-out chessmen, table-tennis paddles and drumsticks. And they adopted all the standard secret-compartment devices of the smuggling trade, among them false-bottomed suitcases, or altered milk churns and beer crates *(left)*.

Microfilming, a relatively new process that was refined by SOE, made concealment much easier. Information that filled nine printed pages could be reduced to a microfilm strip small enough to insert in a hollowed-out matchstick. A microdot no bigger than $\frac{1}{32}$ of an inch could be fastened onto a watch crystal or attached to an eyeglass lens for safekeeping—and later enlarged to reveal secret information up to 500 words in length.

A magnetized bar, balanced on a metal belt buckle, points accurately to the north.

TRAVEL AIDS FOR AGENTS AND RESISTANTS

Many a clandestine operation, from the infiltration of an air-dropped SOE agent to a sabotage mission by a Resistance group, depended upon implements that would guide the bearers on their way but would escape detection if they were searched. Both purposes were served by direction-finding equipment originally designed to help Allied airmen who bailed out over enemy territory: miniature compasses and maps of gossamer thinness.

The maps were printed on small squares of silk so sheer that they could be wrapped inconspicuously around the lead in a mechanical pencil. The compasses—some as small as one eighth of an inch across—could be built into buttons and cuff links, rings and hairbrushes *(left)* and removable gold teeth. One compass consisted of a magnetized razor blade that dangled on a piece of thread; the first letter of the manufacturer's name pointed north.

The Germans who examined the secret travel aids were impressed. One captured German report noted that the compasses were "of simple but perfect construction" and that the maps were "remarkable for their clarity and completeness."

The wooden handle of a hairbrush (top) lifts up to reveal a small, hidden compass (bottom).

A pencil becomes a compass when its clip is balanced on its sharpened point.

An inexpensive cigarette lighter and a common pipe (top) contain ample space for hiding tiny compasses (bottom).

CANNED BOMBS AND LETHAL FOUNTAIN PENS

Resistants and Allied agents possessed an arsenal of exotic weapons to use against the Germans. Most of these implements shared two virtues: they were easy to carry and looked thoroughly harmless.

The chief offensive weapon was made to order for sabotage: a plastic explosive that had the consistency of dough. It could be molded to fit any receptacle, from a briefcase to an empty can. Properly fused, it became a powerful bomb. As little as three pounds of the plastic could blast a hole big enough to sink a ship.

Ballistics experts in Britain offered SOE operatives a variety of unpistol-like pistols. One, often strapped to the leg and called the welrod, fired a single bullet silently. Others masqueraded as mechanical pencils or fountain pens—one of which used phonograph needles as ammunition.

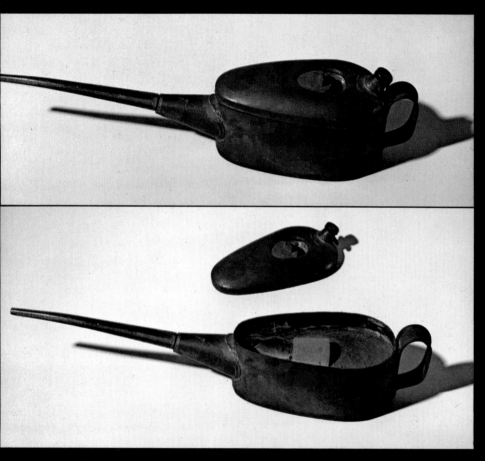

A mechanic's oilcan (top) was the repository of a small, homemade bomb (bottom) that was set off by a delayed-action detonator.

A bicycle pump (below, top) housed a single-shot gun, as did a commonplace mechanical pencil (bottom, left) and a fountain pen.

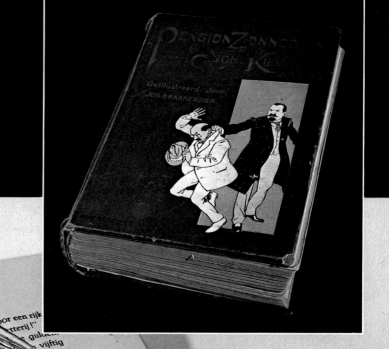

A small revolver was carried by a Dutch resistant inside an ordinary children's book (inset) that had been carefully hollowed out to hold the gun securely.

3

The many underground groups that emerged in France had little in common at first—except determination to take action against the Germans. Each of these networks stubbornly charted its own course, guided by its own aims and opinions of how best to resist. Inevitably, the lack of shared goals limited the effectiveness of the movement, and precious energies were squandered on internecine quarrels.

The need for a coordinating leader or committee was a matter of obsessive concern to a French civil servant named Jean Moulin. Displaying the cool disregard for difficulties that marks an extraordinary man, Moulin undertook a prodigious task that eventually led to the formation of a nationwide resistance organization. He began the job knowing that it might well cost him his life. But he did not fear death; once before, after his first encounter with the Germans, in June of 1940, he had actually chosen to die.

At the time of France's fall, Jean Moulin had been the prefect of the department of Eure-et-Loir, a district just southwest of Paris. Moulin had risen swiftly through the ranks of civil service; he was just 40, the youngest prefect in the country. He had gained a reputation as a gifted administrator, endowed with quiet strength and a magnetic personality. During the terror of the German invasion, Moulin added to this reputation, remaining at his post as others fled southward, setting up aid stations for refugees who streamed through his department, making sure that the wounded were cared for and the dead were buried. His energy and competence worried the Germans who arrived to occupy the department seat, Chartres; they saw in him a potential problem.

And so they set out to break him. Their method was not complicated. Seven women and children in the village of Saint-Georges-sur-Eure had been massacred and mutilated; two German soldiers sent by their commander in Chartres confronted Moulin in his office on June 17 and demanded that he sign a piece of paper accusing French-African soldiers of the deed. There was no evidence to back up the accusation; Moulin realized that signing the document would dishonor the French Army and himself, and he refused. The German soldiers were enraged at his obstinacy. They began beating him and threatened to shoot him on the spot. When violence and threats failed, they tried another tactic. They drove Moulin to a farmhouse where the corpses

JEAN MOULIN'S MISSION

were piled. The shaken prefect examined one torn body after another and guessed that all had been killed in a German bombing raid. Again he refused to sign the paper.

The Germans resumed their beatings, using their fists, flashlights and rifle butts. Then they locked Moulin in a dark hut with the corpse of a woman, and after a few hours transferred him to a private house in Chartres that had been converted into a prison. As he lay on a filthy mattress in an upstairs room, Moulin concluded that he would crack under interrogation the following day. Later he recalled his thoughts: "I know that today I have gone to the limit of my resistance. I know that if it begins again, I will end up by signing." Rather than do that, Moulin picked up a shard of glass from a broken window and cut his throat.

A sentry found him the next morning, drenched in blood, unconscious, barely alive. It turned out that Moulin had nicked an artery without severing it completely. He was taken to a hospital, where doctors stitched his wound and gave him blood transfusions, saving his life. The Germans were taken aback by Moulin's act. They dropped the matter of the massacre, and when Moulin recovered they allowed him to return to the prefecture. Although they tried to keep the affair quiet, word of the prefect's heroism quickly spread through the department, stirring up pride and subversive notions among people who had accepted the humiliation of the German take-over.

Moulin's experience had committed him to fight the Germans in any way he could. At first he opposed them openly. Back in his office, he sent out instructions to all the mayors in his district ordering them not to post German notices in their offices. He blocked every German demand, from the requisitioning of property to the enforcement of the curfew. When he refused to sack officials known to be anti-German, he himself was peremptorily fired, on November 11, 1940. The German commander in Chartres, no doubt anxious to get rid of the troublesome prefect, gave him a pass to cross into the unoccupied zone.

Now that his attempts at open rebellion had been countered by dismissal, Moulin shifted his attention to the unruly horde of underground groups that were springing up all across France. The need for some sort of central control was manifest, but none of the resistance leaders seemed to be capable of uniting all the disparate factions. Outside of France, however, there was Charles de Gaulle, the émigré general whose fiery, eloquent radio speeches from London had brought hope to all patriotic Frenchmen. Moulin was one of those impressed by de Gaulle's authoritative air and stance against the Germans and Vichy. He decided to try to pull the resistance networks together under the banner of de Gaulle.

The obstacles Moulin faced were daunting in both number and nature. If he entered the occupied zone of France he would have to cope with Gestapo plainclothesmen, Abwehr agents, spies and paid French informers, all of whom were operating with the sole aim of smothering internal resistance. Even in the unoccupied zone, he faced the Vichy police and its web of informants, who were just as zealous as the Germans in their efforts to suppress the resistance workers, whom they considered no better than terrorists. Moulin would have to conduct his organizing work underground, in absolute secrecy, in constant danger of betrayal, knowing that one slip could bring arrest, torture and death. And as Moulin fully realized, he could lose a lot more than his life. If his work went well, he would know every important name involved in the resistance. If he were caught and broken under torture, the Germans would have all the information necessary to crush the entire movement.

The local resistance leaders would pose another formidable problem for Moulin. They were supremely egotistical men, ambitious, jealous of one another, often worlds apart politically. Moreover, many of them had gone into hiding, and rivals within their own networks were rising to power. To impose some sort of order on the chaos of the resistance would be a task of Byzantine complexity. Yet Moulin brought to the task several proven assets: persuasiveness, integrity, boundless energy and administrative ability. In time, his use of these assets would make him a figure second in stature in France only to Charles de Gaulle.

The travel pass the Germans had provided gave Moulin exactly what he wanted: freedom of movement. He began journeying throughout southern France, seeking out embryonic resistance cells, judging the worth of their leaders, and taking copious notes.

In the spring of 1941, Moulin's quest brought him into contact with three important, isolated resistance networks:

Libération Nationale, led by Henri Frenay, an energetic Army officer; Liberté, a political group made up largely of Christian Democrats; and Libération, headed by a flamboyant Left-Wing journalist named Emmanuel d'Astier de la Vigerie. Each group published its own clandestine newspaper, clearly reflecting doctrinal and political differences that they had made no serious effort to resolve. Moulin used his charm and tact to persuade each group separately to name him its emissary to Charles de Gaulle—provided, of course, that he could make his way to London to meet the general.

There was one other organization in France with vast potential for resisting the German occupiers: the French Communist Party. But Russia had signed a nonaggression pact with Germany in 1939 and had not yet entered the War. As a result, the French Communists remained aloof from the struggle; they labeled the conflict an imperialist war and referred to de Gaulle as the reactionary aristocrat who had sold out to the British capitalists.

But all that changed on June 22, 1941, when German armies attacked the Soviet Union. With this astounding turn of events, French Communists—like Communists everywhere—performed an abrupt ideological about-face: now the War was no longer an imperialist conflict, but a "democratic war against Fascism" led by the heroic Soviet Union. More important than their new dogma was a swift decision by the party's central committee to back words with action. The principal action they had in mind was the random killing of German soldiers to prevent reinforcements from being sent from France to the Russian front.

A militant young Communist named Pierre-Félix Georges opened hostilities on August 21 by firing two shots into the back of a young German Naval cadet as he was about to step onto a train at the Barbès metro station in Paris. The cadet fell into the train and died with his feet dangling from the door. Georges escaped by running off and shouting "Stop him! Stop him!" after an imaginary assailant.

The next day, red-and-black posters appeared on the streets of Paris with a grim warning:

"On the morning of August 21, a member of the German forces was murdered in Paris. Consequently, by order: (1) Beginning on August 23, all Frenchmen who have been arrested in France . . . will be considered as hostages. (2) In case such an act should happen again, a number of hostages corresponding to the gravity of the crime will be shot."

The Germans did not have to wait very long for an opportunity to make good their threat. The day after the poster appeared, two German officers were killed in Lille, in northeastern France, and the day after that, two more soldiers were shot in the same department. In reprisal, five Communists and three Gaullist agents were yanked out of prison and executed.

On the evening of September 3, 1941, a German officer was shot and seriously wounded in the lobby of Paris' Hôtel Terminus. On the 5th a German military garage in Vincennes was burned down, and the next day another German officer in Paris was killed. Three hostages were executed.

The Communists had known that their actions would provoke reprisals against innocent people and had hoped that widespread revulsion against the executions would swell their ranks. But they could hardly have anticipated the price in French lives that was soon set for that of a single German. On October 21, posters announced a ferocious escalation in the severity of reprisals:

"Cowardly criminals in the pay of England and Moscow have killed, by shooting in the back, the Feldkommandant of Nantes, on the morning of October 20, 1941.

"In expiation of this crime, I have already ordered that 50 hostages be shot. Given the gravity of the crime, 50 more

On the steps of a church in London, General Charles de Gaulle (center) shakes hands with British Foreign Secretary Anthony Eden after a memorial Mass for the 48 French civilians shot on October 24, 1941, in reprisal for the killing of a German official in Nantes four days earlier. De Gaulle broadcast an appeal to occupied France, urging his countrymen to protest the executions: Everyone was "to cease all activity and remain motionless, each wherever he happens to be, on Friday, October 31, from four to four-five." Thousands of Frenchmen did so.

hostages will be shot if the guilty persons are not arrested by midnight, October 23, 1941."

The order was signed by General Heinrich von Stülpnagel, the German military governor in France.

The next day, 27 Communist hostages were driven from a prison camp in Châteaubriant to a sand quarry on the outskirts of town, where they were shot. The same day, in the courtyard of the prison in Nantes in western France, 21 more hostages were executed.

Within 24 hours, yet another 100 hostages were executed in Bordeaux in reprisal for the murder of a German military official. Both Marshal Pétain in Vichy and General de Gaulle in London were alarmed at what was happening, and both broadcast messages of restraint to the nation, although in rather different terms. "We have put down our arms," the old marshal said sternly. "We do not have the right to take them up again to strike the Germans in the back."

General de Gaulle went on the air the following day to say: "It is absolutely natural and absolutely right that Germans should be killed by Frenchmen. If the Germans did not wish to receive death at our hands, they had only to stay at home." For the time being, however, he ordered his ill-armed followers to stop overt killings in order to spare helpless citizens from reprisals. "As soon as we are in a position to move to the attack," he said, "the orders for which you are waiting will be given."

The French Communists refused to take orders from either de Gaulle or Pétain. The killings continued unabated. So did the reprisals.

Jean Moulin, in the meantime, had been preparing for his trip to London. Warned by a friend in government that Vichy did not intend to let him leave France, Moulin set about creating a new identity. Through another friend, he cadged a blank identification card and filled in the fictitious name Joseph Mercier. With the card, he obtained a passport. On September 9, he slipped across the border from France into Spain, and from there he made his way to Lisbon. British authorities in Lisbon interviewed Moulin, immediately recognized his organizing ability and attempted to recruit him into SOE. Presently, word of their efforts reached de Gaulle, who took steps to prevent the loss of a potentially valuable Frenchman to the British intelligence service. He sent a "pressing letter" to Sir Anthony Eden, Secretary of State for Foreign Affairs. At Eden's behest, Moulin was pried loose and sent to London, where he arrived on October 20, 1941. In his brief case was a report he had prepared for de Gaulle on the state of resistance in the southern zone of France.

The general, like everybody else who had come into contact with Moulin, was impressed by his integrity, eloquence and authority. The two men had several lengthy discussions in November and December, during which it was agreed that Moulin should return to France, to organize and unify the resistance movement.

With two associates, Moulin parachuted back into France near Arles on January 1, 1942. He first reestablished contact with Frenay, whose Libération Nationale had recently merged with Liberté to form Combat, the biggest and the best-organized resistance network in France. The two men met in Marseilles, at a little house on the Rue Kléber, and after describing his reception in London, Moulin produced a matchbox. "He opened it," Frenay recalled, "and took out a handful of tiny slips that fit the box's contours exactly. He handed us the first slip—it was a microfilm—along with a magnifying glass. By the light of the small lamp over the gas stove I read 'I hereby appoint Jean Moulin as my personal representative. . . . M. Moulin's mission is to bring about the concerted action of all elements that resist the enemy and the collaboration. M. Moulin is to report to me directly upon the accomplishment of his mission.'" The document was signed "C. de Gaulle."

"Here at last," continued Frenay, "was what we had so long awaited: contact with Free France, miraculous contact on the highest level! What a powerful spur this would be to our unity drive! We read pure joy in one another's faces."

Their joy was short-lived, however, for the other strips of microfilm contained detailed orders from London on how their network should be organized and operated. Frenay and his colleagues were dismayed: they had managed perfectly well thus far; why should they suddenly be required to take orders from London?

Frenay called together Combat's steering committee to ponder whether they should sacrifice their independence in return for London's money, arms, ammunition and other supplies—all desperately needed. After a long discussion, they agreed that Combat would make an effort to carry out de Gaulle's directives.

Moulin was delighted. Raymond Fassin and radio operator Hervé Monjaret—the two men who had returned with him by parachute—were assigned to work with Combat for the rest of the year. They quickly set up an organization that became a vital channel for the delivery of arms and ammunition to the resistance in unoccupied France, and that also arranged for the transport of French agents and politicians between France and England.

Other resistance networks soon fell in line. Moulin met d'Astier, of Libération, in Lyons and leaders of Franc-Tireur, a Catholic resistance group, in Avignon. Traveling by train, bus and bicycle, he moved from town to town, tirelessly spreading the Gaullist word. Almost everywhere he went, he was followed by a courier carrying a second set of false papers, ready to hand them over in case a sudden crisis forced him to change his identity. On March 30, Moulin was able to report to London that all the resistance organizations he had contacted had pledged allegiance to de Gaulle.

Also by March came an unmistakable change in the attitude of ordinary French people toward the German pres-

ence. For nearly two years many citizens in the occupied zone had borne their lot in bitter silence. But now they were becoming restless. Public protests started in Lyons, on the evening of March 18, 1942, when the Berlin Philharmonic Orchestra was due to give a concert. Local resistance groups had distributed leaflets calling for the event to be disrupted, but they could hardly have anticipated just how successful they would be.

By 8 p.m. a huge crowd had assembled in front of the concert hall at the Place des Terreaux. "A police barricade was erected to contain the crowd," one participant wrote, "and anyone who tried to pass through the crowd toward the concert hall was jeered and hissed. Very few attempted it. . . . The fervor of the demonstration was such that it spilled down the main streets. . . . Trams were stopped and fights broke out between demonstrators and police. There were numerous arrests. This was the first great public demonstration of resistance. The result galvanized our activity. We began to have confidence in ourselves."

The news of what had happened in Lyons quickly spread. On May Day there were demonstrations in Nice, Toulouse, Saint-Etienne, Clermont-Ferrand, Avignon, Toulon, Mont-

pellier, Sète and Chambéry, all extensively reported in the underground press. Two months later, in Toulouse, a crowd gathered at the Place du Capitole and sang the "Marseillaise" outside a hall where a German speaker was lecturing.

All this was a prelude to greater demonstrations on Bastille Day, July 14. Clandestine newspapers in each city, backed up by repeated broadcasts from the BBC, published details of the time and place where people should convene. The results were remarkable: 100,000 people on the streets of Lyons, another 100,000 in Marseilles, 15,000 in Toulouse and thousands more in smaller towns. In Saint-Etienne, 20,000 people demonstrated, and *Espoir*, the local underground paper, commented: "For the first time, people felt free to speak their minds."

Deprivation had finally pushed the French beyond the limits of their considerable endurance. Most working people in the towns were hungry. Their wages had been frozen since 1939 (except for a small raise in May 1941), and food prices had, in the meantime, increased as much as 300 per cent. All the staple commodities of French domestic life were in desperately short supply. What luxuries had not been shipped to Germany were available only on the black market at prices that only the Germans could afford.

By now, moreover, few people had any illusions about the nature of the Occupation. The Germans had demanded that 350,000 French workers be sent to factories in Germany to help the war effort. In Paris, 22,000 Jews had been rounded up and herded into the Vélodrome d'Hiver, a sports stadium, to await shipment to concentration camps. In the unoccupied zone, Pétain's Prime Minister, Pierre Laval, had dishonored French patriotism with a broadcast on June 22, 1942. "I desire Germany's victory," he said solemnly, "because only such a victory can save the world from being conquered by Bolshevism."

French morale had been given a big boost that spring by a daring act of sabotage. On the night of May 9, about 30 miles southeast of Paris, a team of SOE saboteurs cut through a fence surrounding a gigantic Radio Paris transmitter that was being used to jam RAF radio traffic. The men were inexperienced and nervous, and they forgot to set time fuses to their charges, as planned, before they cut their way into the station. By the time they had fixed 10 charges to the main pylons of the transmitting tower, the German guards had sounded an alarm and bullets were flying. Under

Rifles at the ready, two Resistance fighters on Corsica, where the term maquis originated, guard an approach to their mountainside hide-out. In September 1943, more than 10,000 maquisards staged a full-fledged armed revolt against the occupiers. Reinforced by French troops from North Africa, the Corsican guerrillas routed their Axis enemies, and on the 3rd of October, 1943, the island became the first part of France to be liberated.

Wearing winter camouflage, members of the Norwegian Home Forces flatten themselves on the snow during training exercises in a remote area of their country. These well-equipped guerrilla fighters, who eventually numbered 50,000 men, were preparing for an operation that never materialized—an Allied invasion of Norway. But far from waiting idly, they committed sabotage and fought hot little skirmishes with German troops.

fire, the three saboteurs quickly set the fuses and made off. Fortunately, the timing devices were defective and detonated the explosives prematurely; had the saboteurs set the fuses as originally planned, they would have blown themselves to pieces. But if their mission had not been cleanly executed, it had been a success. For two weeks the dead silence of the transmitting station attested to the growing strength of the resistance.

By August of 1942, Jean Moulin could report good progress with part of his mission—organizing the resistance. A reception committee, with many branches, had been set up in the occupied zone to receive supplies of arms and ammunition and to send agents back to Britain. A clandestine press agency circulated Allied propaganda in France. And another of Moulin's organizations was tackling the task of penetrating the Vichy administration, recruiting public officials into the resistance and gathering intelligence.

But the prospect of actually unifying resistance networks in the unoccupied zone still seemed as remote as ever. One of Moulin's fundamental aims as a step toward unification was to merge the paramilitary units of the three biggest resistance groups into a "Secret Army" under a single command. The leaders reacted with typical disparity. Jean-Pierre Lévy, of Franc-Tireur, and d'Astier, of Libération, did not object, providing the commander was an outsider who owed no allegiance to any of the major networks. Frenay, of Combat, approved only if he was appointed the commander. Frenay and d'Astier, by themselves, represented a major stumbling block to unity, largely because they heartily detested each other. If they agreed about anything, it was only that Moulin was getting too high-handed.

In an effort to mend the rift, Moulin arranged for Frenay and d'Astier to go to London to lay their problems before de Gaulle. A fishing boat picked them up from the cove of Port-Miou, near Marseilles, on the night of September 14.

From the boat they were transferred to a Royal Navy cruiser, which took them to Gibraltar; then a seaplane flew them to England, where they arrived on September 26.

At the Free French offices in London's Mayfair district, neither man made a particularly favorable impression. André Dewavrin, the head of de Gaulle's intelligence service, the BCRA, described d'Astier contemptuously as "an anarchist in dancing shoes" because of his radical politics and elegant clothes. Frenay, he noted, had a disconcerting habit of expressing contradictory ideas in quick succession, sentiments the intelligence chief dryly referred to as "successive sincerities." Nevertheless, both men had much valuable information to impart, and de Gaulle was happy enough to see them. He was less happy when, in a rare moment of accord, the two resistance leaders demanded removal of Jean Moulin. "The resistance," Frenay declared, "does not need a tutor."

Later Frenay returned to the subject. What would happen, he asked, if the resistance leaders would not reach agreement with Moulin?

Then, de Gaulle replied testily, "France will choose between you and me!"

On the 8th of November, 1942, the Allies launched Operation *Torch,* a massive invasion of French North Africa. In the early hours of that day, some 110,000 U.S. and British troops splashed ashore from nearly 500 ships at Casablanca, Oran and Algiers. The troops established beachheads and soon were launching drives eastward against German forces in North Africa.

Operation *Torch* had a monumental and enduring impact on the resistance movement in France. On November 11 the Germans in France reacted swiftly and decisively to the invasion of North Africa. Wehrmacht troops crossed the demarcation line dividing the two zones of France and occupied the remainder of the country on the pretext of defending the Mediterranean coast. Henceforth, the Vichy government was truly a tool of the Germans. The entire country lay under the heel of the German jackboot, and any remaining delusions that part of France was still free were rapidly extinguished.

At about the same time, the Germans' urgent need to expand their work force was causing a crisis that would push thousands of young men into the ranks of the active underground. Since March, Fritz Sauckel, Hitler's manpower overseer, had been demanding laborers from France to work in German factories. Recruiting offices were opened in both zones, but volunteers were few. Under pressure from Sauckel, Prime Minister Laval had announced in June a scheme called *la relève*—the relief—under which one French prisoner of war would be released for every three Frenchmen volunteering for work in Germany.

This enticement produced some 200,000 volunteers, but the supply soon dried up as news filtered back of the working conditions they encountered. Posters advertising *la relève* in France offered high wages and facilities to send parcels and money home. The reality, as reported succinctly by the Socialist underground newspaper *L'Insurgé*, was rather different: "Journey: long, little food, under German supervision. On arrival: camps where workers treated like cattle. Later: sleeping in barracks, herded together. Work: 12 hours a day, piecework but no increase in wages. Wages: enormous taxes and fines. Cost of living: higher than in France. Food: not even enough for Italians who are used to

Marshal Henri Philippe Pétain (far left), the doddering octogenarian chief of the Vichy regime, once said that "what I have really loved in my life were infantry and love-making." His sinister Vice Premier, Pierre Laval—here seen being escorted to a meeting with Hitler—was single-mindedly interested in power. After his conference with the Führer, Laval crowed: "We felt the same way."

An unenthusiastic Frenchman is congratulated by German officers on becoming the 100,000th worker drafted for labor in Germany. The conscripts—who numbered 600,000 by 1944— often took revenge by sabotaging factories in which they worked, and thousands of them were sent off to concentration camps.

low subsistence. Freedom: nil. Conclusion: exploitation, prisoner status. Thousands of workers killed by bombing."

Vichy made a further attempt to satisfy Sauckel in September by drafting a law to give teeth to la relève. It required all medically fit men between the ages of 18 and 50, and all single women between 21 and 35, to be available for work that the government judged to be "beneficial to the overall interests of the nation." The resistance press immediately denounced the plan, and protest strikes and demonstrations were staged` throughout the country. In Lyons, railway workers struck to delay trains taking workers to Germany. In Limoges, 826 workers out of 830 in a convoy scheduled to leave for the Reich refused to sign papers that declared they were volunteers. In Brive, demonstrations against la relève coincided with the day the Germans occupied Vichy France: troops marching into the town were met by crowds shouting "A bas les Boches!" ("Down with the Boches!"), and sand and gravel were thrown at them.

Despite this clear indication of the temper of the people, Prime Minister Laval forged ahead with a plan to guarantee Germany a regular flow of French workers: he set up a system of forced labor. In February of 1943, he instituted the Service du Travail Obligatoire, a measure requiring all Frenchmen of mobilizable age to report for work in Germany. The law backfired on Vichy. Already quite a few young men had taken refuge in the wild mountain bastions of France to avoid la relève; after February they were joined by labor draft dodgers by the thousands.

In time, these tatterdemalion bands of refugees came to be known as maquis, a word meaning "scrubby underbrush" and associated by bloody tradition with Corsica's mountain thickets, where for centuries outlaws had roamed and raided. The name was apt; the men in most of the maquis led squalid lives in crude mountain hide-outs. In the dismal winter of 1943-1944 they were cold, hungry and hunted. At first they ventured from their brambled citadels mainly in quest of food, for which they begged, stole or killed. Later, as their ranks swelled, the maquisards were supplied by Allied airdrops and joined and trained by regular officers of the disbanded French Army and by Allied agents dropped into their areas. Gradually the scattered maquis were molded into an underground army that played an important role in the struggle for national freedom.

The fugitive maquisards hated the Germans, of course, but they reserved a special loathing for another breed of enemy, a home-grown organization of fellow Frenchmen named the Milice. Formed in the winter of 1943, the Milice was a Vichy police force originally charged with maintaining order in the unoccupied zone. Under the leadership of Joseph Darnand, a zealous Fascist, it became the nationwide equivalent of the dreaded German Gestapo. At the beginning, the Milice had attracted many recruits from the bourgeoisie, citizens appalled by the mounting lawlessness in the land. But as the organization became more desperate in its determination to crush the Resistance, it recruited hoodlums and criminals: Vichy courts even resorted to offering convicted felons the choice of enlisting in the Milice rather than serving a prison term. Murder, rape and pillage became Milice hallmarks.

Darnard made sure that his Miliciens worked hand in hand with the Germans in tracking down the maquis. The maquis fought back with the scathing hatred reserved for those who have turned against their own. Both the maquis and the Milice grew stronger, accumulating weapons and men. In time, the encounters between them would become exercises in savagery.

When the forced-labor law was announced, Moulin was in London. After nearly 14 months in the field, he had been withdrawn for a short rest and to discuss with de Gaulle an ambitious plan to set up the Conseil National de la Résistance, a national council that would represent the leading resistance networks in France. Since Frenay and d'Astier's visit to London, the military coordinating committee in the south had been working well, but in the north there was still little liaison among the biggest networks.

To help Moulin bring together the leading networks in the north, three more men were sent to France from London—André Dewavrin, the head of the Free French intelligence service; his deputy, Pierre Brossolette; and F. F. E. "Tommy" Yeo-Thomas, an SOE agent. The presence of Yeo-Thomas was intended to demonstrate to the French the unity that existed between de Gaulle's Free French and SOE.

By the time Moulin had parachuted back into France, at the end of March, these three men had laid the foundation for unifying the resistance in the north, and at a meeting on

LION-SIZED DEEDS IN A DIMINUTIVE NATION

"You must support everything I decree and you must do so particularly when you do not understand why," announced Deputy Führer Gustav Simon shortly after he was appointed German administrator of Luxembourg in August 1940. It was but one of several irrational demands that led the tiny grand duchy—300,000 strong—to fight its occupation with all the ferocity of Luxembourg's official emblem, the lion.

The real trouble began in August 1942 when Germany annexed the country and ordered men between the ages of 20 and 24 inducted into the German Army. Overnight, thousands of Luxembourgers went underground to avoid conscription, and many were spirited to safety by escape organizations—notably a group that called itself the Luxembourg Red Lions (below).

But the country's Resistance efforts were at least as much help to the Allies as to their own people. An outfit known as the Luxembourg Patriotic League helped some 4,000 Allied airmen and soldiers escape the Nazis. And another group managed the sensational coup of sending the Allies the first description of the secret V-1 rocket installations at Peenemünde in northern Germany; with fitting irony, the information was obtained from a conscripted Luxembourger who was on home leave from guard duty at the site.

Members of a group called the Red Lions assemble in an abandoned iron mine that served as an operations base in southern Luxembourg.

April 12 the leaders of the Organisation Civile et Militaire, Ceux de la Résistance, Ceux de la Libération, Libération-Nord and Front National all agreed to accept directives from de Gaulle in London and to coordinate their activities in line with current Allied strategy. One major disagreement, which was never resolved, centered on the refusal of the Communist Front National to wait for an Allied invasion before launching offensive actions against the occupiers. The Communists reported they were killing 550 Germans a month. Between January and March, 1943, their paramilitary group, the Francs-Tireurs et Partisans, claimed to have mounted 1,500 actions against enemy transport, including 150 derailings, destruction of 180 locomotives carrying war matériel or troops, and sabotage of 110 engines, 14 barges, three bridges and eight canal locks.

Moulin did not choose to make an issue of Communist intransigence, now that formation of the national council was in sight. He was in constant touch with the elements of the embryonic council, and under his tactful direction the remaining problems were being ironed out. Many of the difficulties stemmed from jealousy: leaders of the big resistance movements wanted more than one seat on the new council; smaller networks fretted about loss of prestige and identity; the Communists, claiming they were the only political group actively involved in the resistance, objected to the presence of other political parties. But step by painstaking step, Moulin brought them closer together.

On May 27, 1943, in an apartment at 48 Rue du Four in Paris, Moulin took the chair at the first meeting of the council. Sixteen members were present: eight from resistance groups, six from political parties and two from trade-union federations. Moulin opened the proceedings with a statement of aims as defined by General de Gaulle: (1) to continue the war; (2) to return to the French people freedom of speech and civil rights; (3) to restore republican liberty and social justice in a state "that will have the sense of grandeur"; (4) to work with the Allies for "real international collaboration . . . in a world where French prestige is acknowledged by all." The council members then voted to put their faith in de Gaulle; after three years of German occupation, the French Resistance was finally united. And Jean Moulin, the man who had achieved that unification, was moving inexorably toward his own destruction.

The key had turned on Moulin's fate exactly a month before. On the 27th of April, during a routine street check in Marseilles, the Gestapo had picked up Jean Multon (alias "Lunel"), the second-in-command of Combat's Marseilles cell. Threatened with torture and reprisals, Lunel broke and agreed to work for the Gestapo. Once he had switched sides, he was sent out day after day to find his former friends. With two German agents always at his side, Lunel haunted the cafés and restaurants of Marseilles in which he knew resistants met, indicating with a nod of his head the men to be arrested. Before word of his treachery had spread, 125 members of the underground in Marseilles were in the hands of the Gestapo. Frenay ordered Lunel's immediate execution, but by then the traitor had been moved to Lyons, to continue his infamous duties there.

Lunel's first task in Lyons was to monitor a "letter box" the Gestapo had discovered on the Rue Bouteille. Letter box was the term for a safe address where resistants could deliver or collect messages; the Germans had been told that this one was being used by the head of Combat's railway sabotage unit, a man they knew only by his code name, "Didot."

Didot was René Hardy, a young railway engineer who

Resistance hero Jean Moulin, who unified the many contentious underground groups in France, used a longtime hobby—drawing—to taunt the Germans after he was captured in 1943. Moulin withstood torture for days without betraying his comrades. Though badly battered, he then defiantly drew a vicious caricature of the Gestapo officer who had been orchestrating his ordeal, and presented the sketch to its subject.

already had been credited with directing or controlling more than 550 railway attacks, resulting in the destruction of nearly 300 locomotives. He was also an important contributor to *Plan Vert,* an extraordinarily detailed document of 150 pages containing plans in code for sabotage at thousands of railway stations and crossings. The wily Didot was a top priority target for the Gestapo in Lyons, although none of the Germans knew what he looked like. Lunel, who did, was assigned to finger him.

Hardy did not fall into the trap set for him on the Rue Bouteille because, as he later testified, he had abandoned the letter box after learning of the arrests in Marseilles following Lunel's treachery. Instead, the Gestapo bagged quite another prize. While Lunel was watching the letter box, a message was delivered there for Didot; the note instructed Didot to meet ''Vidal'' at the entrance to La Muette metro station in Paris at 9 a.m. on June 9. The Gestapo was delighted: Vidal was General Charles Delestraint, who had been chosen by de Gaulle to lead the paramilitary wing of the Resistance, the Secret Army.

What happened next was later viewed by many resistants as one piece of evidence—one among many—that Hardy, too, had turned traitor, although it was never proved in a court of law. At the Lyons station on the evening of June 7, 1943, Hardy boarded the night train for Paris, where he was to attend a meeting to organize railroad sabotage. In an adjoining compartment, by amazing coincidence, sat Lunel, accompanied by his German protectors. At some point early in the journey, the two men recognized each other, yet Hardy inexplicably made no attempt to leave the train at any of the stops. At 1 o'clock the following morning, while the train was halted at Chalon-sur-Saône, Hardy was arrested and hauled off to the local prison. He was picked up there later by Klaus Barbie, head of the Lyons Gestapo, who had felt it worthwhile to make the 70-mile journey to Chalon just for that purpose.

General Delestraint, meanwhile, was encountering some difficulty in adapting to the unfamiliar demands of clandestine life after a conventional career in the Army. He had shown up at a safe house in Paris, where he was due to spend the night, but he could not remember the password and was therefore denied entry. He checked into a nearby hotel instead, foolishly registering under his own name. At 9 o'clock on the morning of June 9, following instructions, he was outside La Muette metro station. When two men approached and asked if he was waiting for Didot, the general unwisely said yes. They explained they had been sent to fetch him, escorted him to a waiting car and drove him straight to 84 Avenue Foch, the headquarters of the Paris Gestapo. One of his two captors was Lunel.

In Lyons, Klaus Barbie's interrogation of René Hardy was brief—at 11 p.m. on June 10 Hardy was released, having apparently convinced the Gestapo he was innocent of any involvement with the Resistance. His unexpected freedom created its own problems. Anyone let go so quickly was immediately suspect: too many resistants had paid for their release from the clutches of the Gestapo by betraying their friends. Hardy solved the problem by saying nothing about being arrested—he told his colleagues he had escaped arrest by jumping from the train after seeing Lunel.

Two days later, Max Heilbronn, an engineer who had helped Hardy with *Plan Vert,* was arrested in Lyons. He and Hardy had met on a street corner, strolled a few blocks together, then separated. Heilbronn was caught by the Gestapo before he had crossed another block.

Delestraint's arrest was a bitter blow to Jean Moulin. He convened an urgent meeting of national-council members involved in the Secret Army to discuss the appointment of a successor. Though the leaders of the three big underground movements in the south—Frenay, d'Astier and Lévy—were all in London, Moulin was afraid that any delay in naming a replacement for Delestraint would only allow old rivalries to surface. André Lassagne, a native of Lyons, was told to find a suitable place to hold the emergency meeting. The time was fixed for 2 o'clock on the afternoon of Monday, June 21, 1943.

Frenay was to be represented at the meeting by his deputy Henri Aubry, and Aubry was none too happy about it. He knew his boss wanted to command the Secret Army and he was reluctant to take the responsibility of voting anyone else into the job. To support his arguments at the meeting, he decided to recruit the help of a friend: he asked René Hardy if he would come along.

Lassagne arranged for the meeting to be held in the home of an old school friend, Dr. Frederic Dugoujon, who lived in a large white house at the Place Castellane in Caluire, a hilly suburb in north Lyons. A doctor's house was normally a good place for resistants to meet, because people entering and leaving did not attract undue attention.

Aubry, who did not know where the house was, had agreed to join Lassagne 15 minutes before the meeting at the foot of the cable railway in Lyons. Lassagne was surprised to find Hardy waiting with Aubry, but he raised no objection. At Dr. Dugoujon's house, a maid showed them to a first-floor bedroom, where two council members were already waiting. Moulin and two men he was bringing were 45 minutes late. They had just come through the door when the Gestapo burst in, led by a triumphant Klaus Barbié.

Barbié herded everyone into one room, then took over the doctor's dining room to interrogate the prisoners one by one. He knew he had captured de Gaulle's emissary, but he did not know which one was Moulin. When repeated questioning failed to identify Moulin, Barbié tore the leg off a table and began to beat the prisoners with it. Still they remained silent.

Finally Barbié ordered them to be taken away. As they were being led out of the house, Hardy, whose guard had been holding him with a knotted rope twisted round his right wrist, tore himself free and escaped. He was the only one of them not handcuffed. A few days later, one other man arrested at Caluire managed to get away from the Germans. After suffering Gestapo torture, Raymond Aubrac, a member of the military coordinating committee in the north, was rescued in Lyons when a Resistance group ambushed a German truck in which he was riding. Aubrac's wife, Lucie, planned the ambush and led it with a Tommy gun in her hand, despite being more than eight months pregnant. A few weeks later, an RAF Lysander plane flew the Aubracs out of France. Madame Aubrac went into labor on the flight to England and gave birth to her baby shortly after arriving.

The arrests at Caluire left the leadership of the French Resistance in a shambles. Moulin had not found it easy to delegate authority, preferring instead to hold all the reins; nor had he troubled to train anyone to succeed him. The organization he had set up remained, to a large extent, intact but headless. Both Brossolette and Yeo-Thomas were in London, and unable to assume control. It was left to a secretary to inform London by radio of the disaster at Caluire. And Moulin's young assistant, Claude Serreulles, who had parachuted into France only a few days before, was obliged to try picking up the pieces.

During the second week in July it was decided in London that Brossolette and Yeo-Thomas should return to France to assess the damage and to help Serreulles rebuild what they could from the ruins. But their departure was delayed for more than two months by a bitter quarrel between SOE and the Gaullists.

The dispute began when the Free French proposed to send a message to the field appointing two *chefs de zone*, each to control resistance in half of France. At the time, the SOE chiefs were pressing for the Resistance to be decentralized to avoid the risk of another Caluire, and they objected to the new appointments. The French apparently acquiesced; they submitted a new, differently encoded message for review before transmission, assuring their British counterparts that the appointments had been left out.

That might have been the end of the matter had not an observant SOE officer noticed that the new message had the same number of letter groups as the first. An afternoon's work by SOE's deciphering section cracked the code and revealed that the contents of the two telegrams were identical. The British were furious at this French duplicity and the French were furious that the British had somehow obtained their codes. While the row lasted, junior officers from both sides attempting to maintain contact with their men in the field had to meet in pubs and on street corners, since they were officially forbidden to enter each other's offices.

Brossolette and Yeo-Thomas did not arrive back in France until September 19. Two days after landing near Angoulême in southwestern France, they had their first meeting with Claude Serreulles in an apartment in a fashionable quarter of Paris. Both were immediately alarmed by the young man's offhand confidence and lack of security—and their fears were corroborated by Serreulles' arrest before the week was out. He managed to talk his way out of trouble, but a subsequent raid on his apartment netted the Germans a list of 14 proposed members of a reconstituted national council. Many more arrests followed.

Spurred by these successes, the Gestapo hunters were relentless during the month of October. Yeo-Thomas and Brossolette came within inches of capture. Yeo-Thomas later wrote, "In spite of the energetic tightening up of security . . . the tempo of arrests seemed to accelerate; it was like a landslide." On two occasions, agents whom they had met were arrested within an hour of the time that the meeting broke up. Once, after dining in a house they considered safe, Brossolette and Yeo-Thomas felt unaccountably uneasy and left; the Gestapo raided the house that night and arrested their hostess. Yeo-Thomas was trailed a number of times, but he eluded his pursuers by plunging into a convenient crowd, or by hopping off a metro train and diving back on just as the doors closed.

Once, Yeo-Thomas wrote, he and Brossolette had an appointment with a Gaullist agent whose code name was Necker. "We met him and noticed that he was being trailed by no less than three men. He had not realized it and would not believe us, so we proved it by walking fast, turning down Rue d'Argenson and again onto Rue de la Boétie and waiting just round the corner in a big arched doorway; one by one our three followers came tearing round the corner and left us in no doubt as to their intentions. We then doubled back on our tracks and made rapid plans to dodge our unwelcome friends. We sent Necker off on his own onto the Rue Laborde before the three sleuths could come back on us—Brossolette and I then walked briskly toward Place St. Augustin and agreed to separate and meet an hour later at the corner of Avenue de Villiers and Boulevard de Courcelles. As we arrived at Place St. Augustin we saw two *vélo-taxis* and each jumped into one, thus leaving our followers with no means of catching us up."

Despite the proximity of the Gestapo, Yeo-Thomas and Brossolette continued their work, smoothing over squabbles and setting the conflicts that had developed within the Resistance hierarchy in the absence of Jean Moulin. By the end of October, they had succeeded in negotiating a compromise, and the national council was reconstituted under the chairmanship of Georges Bidault, a young and highly respected member of Combat. The reins of the French Resistance were in firm hands once again—and permanently this time. Thus Yeo-Thomas and Brossolette had placed the capstone on the achievement of their remarkable friend, Jean Moulin.

Moulin's last contact with the Resistance came in the Lyons prison where he had been taken after his arrest at Caluire. On June 24, Christian Pineau, a member of a Socialist Resistance group who had been arrested earlier, was called from his cell and ordered to shave an unconscious man stretched out in the prison courtyard while a German soldier stood guard. "Imagine my horror when I recognized the man stretched out on the bench as none other than Moulin," Pineau wrote later. "He had lost consciousness; his hollow eyes seemed to be sunken in his head. There was an ugly bluish wound on his temple. A soft, rasping sound escaped from his swollen lips. Without doubt, he had been tortured by the Gestapo."

When Pineau began to shave him, Moulin regained consciousness. Pineau recalled: "Suddenly, he opened his eyes and looked at me. I'm certain that he recognized me, but how could he understand my presence before him at that moment? 'Drink' he murmured. I turned toward the soldier: '*Ein wenig wasser.*' He hesitated for an instant, then took the cup filled with soapy water, went to rinse it at the fountain, and brought it back filled with fresh water. During that time, I leaned over him, whispering some banal words of comfort, stupid words. He said five or six words in English which I could not understand, his voice being so badly broken, so gasping. Then he drank several swallows from the cup that I held for him and fainted again."

Eventually Moulin was driven to Paris and put up for a time in a house occupied by a high-ranking SS officer. From there he was placed on a train bound for Germany. It has never been established with certainty when or where he died. But the terrible burden of silence that Moulin imposed upon himself undoubtedly contributed to his death. For Jean Moulin revealed nothing of what he knew about the French Resistance before he died. And as the man who gave it unity, he knew virtually everything.

THE COLLABORATORS

French collaborators mingle with German officers at a swearing-in ceremony for new members of the Milice, a French security force that fought the Resistance.

MIXED MOTIVES FOR AIDING THE OCCUPIERS

To patriots in occupied Europe, one of the most distasteful words in any language was "collaborator." Many Europeans were driven into the ranks of the Resistance not so much by the German conquerors as by their countrymen who hurried forward to help the occupiers. As a Frenchwoman explained with bitter vehemence, "Defeat we could accept; collaboration, never!"

The collaborators who made that name anathema stigmatized themselves publicly with their cynicism and self-seeking. They were the leaders of the puppet governments; the anti-Semites, opportunists and thugs who volunteered for national security forces; the publishers who put a Nazi slant on the news in exchange for German subsidies; the authors, artists and entertainers who used their skills for the benefit of the German Ministry of Propaganda. Some 300,000 people in occupied France alone were indicted after the War for such deeds.

A much larger number of people collaborated in lesser ways, mostly just to survive. Women consorted with German soldiers. Unemployed laborers took jobs in factories churning out vital parts for the German war machine. Minor officials executed German orders to keep their posts. But a little cooperation was a dangerous thing, particularly in officialdom: Even if a man played along in hopes of being able to soften German policy, one compromise or concession often led to another, and another—and soon to full-blown collaboration. Recalled one member of the Vichy government, "I saw men change and become corrupt. You could see before your eyes all the courage and loyalty that you knew to exist in someone melt away, crumble and disappear."

As the fortunes of war turned against the Germans, the ranks of collaborators dwindled down to a hard core of men who had burned their bridges behind them. In desperation, these collaborators—some of them well-intentioned souls four years before—struck out harder and harder against their countrymen who had taken the Resistance route. They earned a name even worse than collaborator: traitor.

Welcoming the invaders to a Belgian village, a resident proudly displays the Iron Cross he won in World War I, when the area was part of Germany.

A group of young Frenchmen ponder a poster urging them to join the French division of Germany's Waffen-SS—the military arm of Hitler's security apparatus.

Decked out in an expensive fur, a Frenchwoman enjoys a beverage with her German companion—the official in charge of the labor draft in Nice, France.

REWARDING DALLIANCES WITH THE CONQUERORS

In Denmark, the local women who offered companionship and sexual favors to lonely German soldiers were contemptuously referred to as "field mattresses," and in other occupied countries, they drew worse epithets from angry patriots.

Even if such women were fully aware of the insults, however, they were plentiful offsetting advantages to having a German soldier for a special friend. He could help a woman avoid Occupation regulations and make her difficult existence easier by providing her with extra ration coupons. He could generally afford the cost of taking her out to restaurants, theaters and music halls.

In addition to that, many women fell for the tough and handsome demeanor of some of the conquerors. One admirer, the daughter of a French industrialist, gushed that the Germans, "with their stern regard, their boots, their swelling chests and blond hair," represented "a world in which suddenly I wanted to live, a world of force, of beauty, of virility."

A merry Dutchwoman sports with a German officer in an Amsterdam café.

A Danish woman chats with her German friend at a lake in Copenhagen. It was a new romance; just three months earlier, the Germans had seized Denmark.

A juvenile member of the Nationalist-Socialist Youth of Flanders stands at attention before older boys of the Belgian league.

A youthful follower of Pétain, standing beneath the marshal's poster portrait, peddles buttons bearing the Vichy coat of arms to raise money for a national welfare fund.

TRAINING TOMORROW'S PRO-GERMAN LEADERS

In each occupied country, German followers set up a number of youth groups modeled on the Hitler Jugend, the Nazi Party's organization for German boys and girls under the age of 18. The local organizations offered non-Jewish youngsters an apportunity to compete in sports and do worthwhile social work. But their chief purpose was to indoctrinate the boys and girls in Nazi or German-approved dogma and prepare them to lead collaborationist roles in military or government service.

In Norway, Denmark, Holland and Belgium, only a tiny percentage of the eligible youths signed up. In France, however, the indoctrination groups were more successful, partly because most of them preached a home-grown variety of Fascism rather than German Nazism.

The avowed purpose of The Companions of France—a Vichy-based group for boys—was "to teach the adolescent youth of France to live with discipline" and to revere their collaborationist leader, Marshal Pétain. Another group, the Youth of France and Overseas, was less idealistic: it bluntly told its members that they were to fight the British and hate the Jews.

Norwegian youths, recruiting young volunteers for Nazi work camps, explain the labor program to curious German soldiers and local teenagers. Youths staffed agricultural and construction projects in Norway.

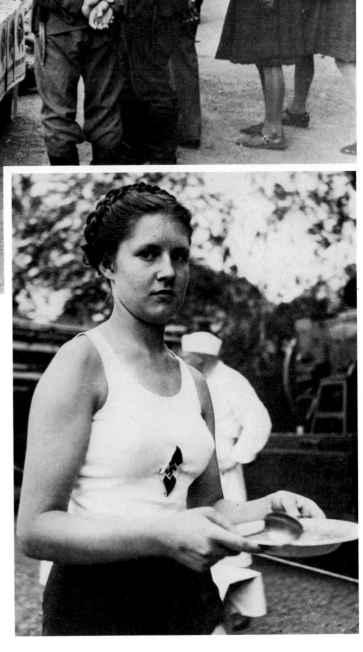

A competitor in a sports festival sponsored by Belgian Nazis in June 1942 stops to have lunch. Youth organizations in every occupied country devoted a huge amount of time and propaganda to physical fitness.

Norwegian volunteers in Russia relax in a bunker under a picture of Norway's top Nazi, Quisling.

Belgian SS troops parade past saluting civilians before they depart for combat duty in the east.

Men of the Legion of French Volunteers Against

Bolshevism receive decorations during a ceremony in Paris in August 1943. The men had spent the year fighting Communist guerrillas in the Soviet Union.

FOREIGN LEGIONS FOR THE FÜHRER

As early as 1940, with the taste of defeat still in their mouths, demobilized soldiers of the occupied countries began enlisting to fight side by side with their conquerors.

Frustrated and bitter, volunteers filled the ranks of several divisions of the elite Waffen-SS. And in late June of 1941, when the Führer invaded the Soviet Union, anti-Communists turned out to join new German units formed to fight on the Russian front. In all, nearly 50,000 men from the occupied areas fought for Hitler.

Volunteers were paid well for service in Hitler's armies. But for some professional soldiers, the real reward was a chance to fight again. Said a French artilleryman in the SS: "Who is right or who is wrong is not, for me, the important thing. It is simply to have a battery of guns under my command once more."

97

A detachment of the French Milice—scourge of the Resistance—parades down the Champs-Elysées in Paris in 1944. More than 40,000 men joined the force.

THOSE WHO FOUGHT THEIR OWN COUNTRYMEN

Practically every citizen nurtured a special terror and hatred for those collaborators who took up arms against their own people. Such individuals were much appreciated by the Occupation authorities, however: as natives, they were better able than the Germans to detect strangers, to spot any suspicious happenings in their home districts and to infiltrate Resistance net-works. And they did their duty with re-morseless dedication.

In Denmark a group of about 400 toughs called the Schalburg Corps dealt so ruth-lessly with members of the Resistance that the Danes coined a versatile new verb: *Schalburgtage,* which meant to kill, rob or destroy. Holland had three notorious police units: the Nazi Landwacht corps, the Henneicke Column, whose specialty was tracking down Jewish fugitives, and a network of so-called V-men—undercover agents who succeeded in worming their way into several Dutch Resistance groups.

But if laurels had been awarded for pure savagery, they would have gone to two infamous French outfits with overlapping franchises—the Milice and the French Self-Defense Corps, both largely manned by native Fascist thugs and released jailbirds. Together, this pair of huge and motley for-ces helped the Gestapo round up more than 8,000 Jews for deportation. And, after applying preliminary torture, they slaugh-tered hundreds of men and women who had served the Resistance.

A Danish terrorist belonging to a branch of the Schalburg Corps mercilessly pounds a fellow citizen. This snapshot was taken hastily by a 15-year-old boy.

At an elaborately staged Nazi rally in Holland, several thousand supporters give the party salute as Dutch leaders wend their way forward to address the crowd.

4

On an RAF mission over the north of France in mid-1941, Flying Officer Alex Nitelet got into a vicious dogfight with several German fighters. His Spitfire was riddled, and he suffered a bullet wound in his right eye; nevertheless, Nitelet somehow managed to crash-land his damaged plane not far from the village of Renty in the Calais area, only 50-odd miles across the Channel from Dover. The young Belgian-born pilot was lucky on two counts. Not only had he survived the crash, but he had landed practically in the lap of an underground organization that already had routed several hundred other downed airmen on a roundabout, 3,500-mile journey back to England.

After struggling clear of his wrecked plane, Nitelet was picked up by a local resistant named Norbert Fillerin, who arranged for a doctor to treat his wound. As soon as he was fit to travel, Nitelet was handed over to another patriot, known only as Didery, who ordered false identity cards and travel documents from a secret printing press run by a Catholic priest in the nearby town of Abbeville. Thus equipped, Nitelet was led by a succession of guides to Paris and thence to the southern city of Marseilles. In Marseilles, Nitelet—following instructions—made his way to a café called Le Petit Poucet. After his identity was confirmed, Nitelet was escorted by one Louis Nouveau to the home of another doctor, who tended the pilot's still-painful wound and hid him for 10 days. From Marseilles, Nitelet traveled by train to the town of Perpignan, where Spanish guides met him and led him over the Pyrenees into Spain. He finally reached London in November 1941, about five months after he was shot down.

The rescue of Nitelet was the work of a difficult and narrowly focused type of resistance operation known as an escape line. People involved in this work specialized in guiding "evaders" (downed airmen and soldiers trapped behind enemy lines) and "escapers" (prisoners of war and captured resistance agents who had broken out of jails and detention camps) to safety beyond the reach of the Occupation forces. It was difficult work; among other things, the escorts were constantly jeopardized in their long journeys by their helpless wards, almost none of whom could even speak the language of the country. Nevertheless, the number of fighting men they saved ran into the thousands, and the importance of the escape lines began to grow enor-

SECRET ROADS TO FREEDOM

mously as the increasingly intensive Allied air raids on Germany deposited more and more downed airmen in Holland, Belgium and France.

In the case of Alex Nitelet, the resistance workers won more than mere gratitude for their efforts. On his return to England, Nitelet learned that his eye wound would bar him from further flying. He immediately volunteered to return to France as a radio operator for the remarkable organization that had arranged his escape, and his offer was promptly accepted by James Langley of MI 9, the branch of British intelligence that was charged with supporting and organizing escape lines.

MI 9, founded in September 1939 under Colonel Norman Crockatt, was a junior member of the British intelligence family. For communications and transportation, it was totally dependent on arrangements made by older or larger services—such as MI 6, the foreign intelligence service, and SOE. Its task of returning British soldiers and airmen trapped behind enemy lines was administered from London by a tiny, top-secret section squirreled away in the War Office's Room 900, a closet-sized office that had formerly served as a tearoom for another secret service. "In the world of military intelligence," said one resident of Room 900, "we were extremely small beer."

The leaders of MI 9 were intimately acquainted with the techniques of escape and evasion in foreign fields. Besides Langley, who had escaped from German-occupied France in 1940, the staff included a well-known World War I escapee named A. J. Evans and—after May 1942—Captain Airey Neave who, having been captured by the Germans at Calais in 1940, walked out of a prisoner-of-war camp and managed to make his way back to England. In addition to the London section, MI 9 had two key undercover agents operating on the Iberian Peninsula. Michael Creswell, the second secretary at the British embassy in Madrid, picked up the fugitives on the Spanish side of the Pyrenees and relayed them by car and bus to Gibraltar, where Donald Darling interrogated them and made all of the arrangements for their return to England.

Through Darling and Creswell, the London staff of MI 9 was able to funnel small amounts of money to the so-called Pat O'Leary Line, which had brought out Alex Nitelet. But communications with the Marseilles-based O'Leary organization were tenuous, sometimes consisting of messages smuggled across the Pyrenees in tubes of toothpaste.

Thus, Alex Nitelet's offer to return to France as a radio operator for the O'Leary Line provided MI 9 with an unexpected solution to the communications problem. The ex-pilot was spirited back into France in May 1942 aboard a Lysander operated by the RAF's secret Moon Squadron (pages 44-45) and eventually he made his way to the Marseilles apartment of Louis Nouveau—one of the agents who had abetted his escape the previous year.

The namesake and boss of the Pat O'Leary Line, Nitelet soon discovered, was a fellow Belgian whose real name was Albert-Marie Guérisse. Guérisse had joined the Belgian cavalry as a medical officer in 1940, had escaped to England after the Germans overran his country and had then volunteered to work for SOE. His first assignment was aboard a Royal Navy ship carrying out clandestine operations along the coast of southern France. During a night landing in April 1941, Guérisse was accidentally left behind and arrested by French coast guards, who interned him in a camp for British prisoners at Nîmes. Several months later he escaped, made his way to Marseilles and linked up with Ian Garrow, a Scottish officer who—despite his imperfect French—had established an escape line to rescue soldiers left behind after the British evacuation from Dunkirk. In October 1941, Garrow was captured and imprisoned by French Vichy police, and Guérisse took charge of the escape line under the nom de guerre of Patrick Albert O'Leary.

Under O'Leary's leadership, the line soon spread a net of more than 250 helpers throughout France. Louis Nouveau was a former stockbroker from Marseilles who had contributed much of his personal fortune to the escape-line funds. The other workers included the Abbé Carpentier in Abbeville, who had supplied Alex Nitelet with false identity papers printed on his own press; a man named Rafarrin, the plump and genial chef on the Paris-Marseilles express train, who doubled as O'Leary's courier between those cities; the Misses Trenchard, two elderly Scottish ladies who ran a tea shop in Monte Carlo and regularly fed evaders hidden in a nearby rented villa; Paul Ulmann, a Jewish tailor from Toulouse who fashioned the clothing O'Leary's operators and clients needed for disguise; Mademoiselle Françoise Dissart, a gray-haired woman of 60 who was O'Leary's principal organizer in Toulouse; and Madame Mongelard, *patronne* of the gloomy, run-down Hôtel de Paris in Toulouse, where the rooms were regularly occupied by fugitives from the Gestapo and the Vichy police.

With the arrival of Alex Nitelet in May 1942, O'Leary at last could put into operation a plan hatched by Langley, Darling and himself during a secret meeting held in Gibraltar the previous April. To avoid the arduous mountain crossing into Spain and the difficult journey across that nominally neutral but actually pro-German country to Gibraltar, O'Leary's evaders would be able now to wait on appointed nights on quiet beaches along the southern coast of France, where a Royal Navy trawler, which would operate out of

Gibraltar and be notified by radio, would pick them up.

In preparation for these amphibious operations, O'Leary's agents rented a small villa at the seaside hamlet of Canet-Plage, near Perpignan, for use as a safe house where evaders could wait undetected for the trawler. With Nitelet coordinating the landing by radio, 35 evaders were safely evacuated from the beach at Canet-Plage in July 1942. Among them was Squadron Leader Whitney Straight, a famous American racing driver who had joined the RAF as a pilot and had been shot down while attacking German submarines near Le Havre. While passing through Rouen on his way south, Straight had spent a couple of pleasant, prankish hours dropping British pennies into the mailboxes of houses with signs announcing the Germans had commandeered them.

All told, O'Leary's agents evacuated six batches of evaders from Canet-Plage and two from other beaches. The final evacuation, in October of 1942, misfired because of a mix-up over the rendezvous point, but was rescheduled and successfully executed, returning 32 more airmen to England. By the autumn of 1942, the rescues carried out by the line had produced a palpable change in the attitude of Britain's Air Ministry toward MI 9.

Until then, the Air Ministry had failed to realize the full potential of the escape lines. When a plane was lost on a mission over enemy territory, the Air Ministry had written off the crew as missing in action—either dead or destined to spend the remainder of the War in a German prison camp. But as the RAF, soon joined by the U.S. Army Air Forces, accelerated the strategic bombing of German war industries, the loss of highly trained aircrews began to be a serious problem. Replacements were expensive: The Air Ministry had to spend £10,000 (about $40,000) to train a bomber pilot, £15,000 for a fighter pilot. More important, the return of airmen thought to be dead or captured was a powerful tonic for flier morale. "We were ordered to re-double our efforts," remembered MI 9's James Langley, "and at last were promised all the moral and material support we so badly needed."

Meanwhile, many new escape lines had sprung up on the Continent without the support of MI 9—and in some cases without its knowledge. One such line was started by an English Red Cross nurse named Mary Lindell, who had married the Comte de Milleville and settled in Paris. The Comtesse had begun in August of 1940 by escorting Captain James Windsor-Lewis of the Welsh Guards across the demarcation line separating German-occupied and Vichy France. Once they were safely out of German territory, the Comtesse put the British officer aboard a train to Marseilles. He eventually made his way to neutral Portugal and caught a flying boat for home. After several other successes, she was captured and imprisoned by the Gestapo. A year and a half later, the Comtesse escaped across the Spanish border in the guise of a stranded English governess and made her way to England.

In London, the indomitable Comtesse enlisted in MI 9, and in October 1942 she returned to France to establish an escape line based in the city of Lyons. Still operating with little or no help from London, she was responsible for the return of some 15 airmen and soldiers, including the only two survivors of a daring British Commando raid that damaged seven German ships in Bordeaux harbor in December 1942. But in late 1943, the Gestapo again caught up with the Comtesse, and she spent the remainder of the War in a French prison and the Ravensbrück concentration camp.

The largest and most successful escape line was one that transported about 1,000 downed airmen, escaped prisoners of war and resistance workers in three years of operation. The line made its debut in August 1941 when a 24-year-old Belgian nurse's aide named Andrée de Jongh—Dédée, to all who knew her—turned up at the British consulate in Bil-

A Dutch Resistance forger, surrounded by the tools and products of his surreptitious trade, painstakingly traces an official signature onto a bogus identity document. More than a half-dozen forged items—ranging from identity cards to travel passes—might be needed by escape-line workers and their Allied charges in order to pass routine and random police checkpoints. Escape-line forgers boasted that they could turn out a faithful copy of any new type of document within three days of its first issue.

Suspiciously eyeing a street photographer who caught him unawares, Patrick O'Leary (the nom de guerre of Albert-Marie Guérisse) strolls through Marseilles in 1941, shortly after taking command of the escape line that bore his name. During four years of operation, the O'Leary Line evacuated some 600 Allied airmen and soldiers from occupied Europe. But 100 escape workers died in concentration camps, and O'Leary himself barely survived two years of imprisonment and torture.

bao on Spain's northern coast. Dédée, dressed in a simple blouse and skirt and wearing white bobby socks, told the astonished vice-consul that she had brought three fugitives with her from Brussels—two young Belgians and a British soldier who had been stranded in Saint Valéry after Dunkirk. With the aid of a Basque guide, they had crossed the Pyrenees on foot the night before. Dédée calmly offered to bring out more British troops from northern France and Belgium. She made a modest request for assistance: would the consul kindly reimburse her for the railway tickets and the guide's fees? He would indeed.

When Dédée returned to Bilbao with another party of evaders two months later, MI 9's Michael Creswell was waiting at the British consulate. He informed Dédée that he would serve as MI 9's Spanish liaison officer for the new line—but he soon realized that she was determined to do things her way. Unlike O'Leary, who at that time was sending his evaders and escapers across the Spanish border from Vichy France, the shrewd young woman ran her whole route through German-occupied France (map, page 108), defying all the attendant risks of tighter Gestapo security and German guards at the Spanish border. Clearly unreceptive to advice, Dédée told Creswell that, apart from money, she would accept no help from MI 9; her line was a Belgian operation, and she wanted no radio operators from London to give the Germans a fix on her position.

Because Dédée referred to the airmen whom she rescued as "packages," Creswell first code-named her line "Postman." But in 1942, when Dédée rushed an entire British bomber crew all the way to Spain in only one week, the name was changed to the more fitting "Comet." Even as her line expanded, Dédée continued working in the field; she personally escorted more than 100 escapers to safety on 32 trips through the rugged Pyrenees. One of her rescued airmen was a 20-year-old RAF pilot named John Hoskins. His account of his experiences on the Comet Line testifies to the daring and efficiency of Dédée's operation.

The hardest part of Hoskins' journey occurred before the Comet Line found him. When his Wellington bomber was hit by flak while returning from a night raid on the Ruhr in September 1942, Hoskins bailed out and landed in the northeastern corner of Belgium. Hiding by day and traveling by night, he headed west in the hope of reaching the coast and stealing a boat to row across the Channel. "At the end of the third night," Hoskins later recalled, "I was looking for a suitable place to hide when an old man came round the corner of the lane on a bicycle. We had been told that if something like this happened, we should act nonchalant. The only nonchalant thing I could think to do was to stroll past him and say 'Guten morgen, mein herr'—about the only German I knew."

The old man recognized Hoskins' RAF uniform and led him to Loksbergen, a small village in Flanders, where everyone was eager to help him. Through a woman who could speak French, Hoskins learned that it was virtually impossible to escape by way of the Channel coast, which was heavily patrolled. He was advised to head instead for Marseilles by train. The villagers brought him civilian clothes, collected money to pay for his ticket and triumphantly escorted him to the railway station.

By the end of the day, Hoskins had reached Namur, near the French border. There he disembarked from the train and then hurried out of town to avoid being picked up for violating the curfew. As he left the houses behind, Hoskins saw another old man in a field digging potatoes. "We had been told," he recalled, "that if we had to make contact with locals, we should choose older, poorer people because they were more likely to be sympathetic. So I went up to him and said in French, 'Good evening, monsieur. I am an English aviator. Please help me!' "

The man led Hoskins to his farmhouse, where his wife cooked up a marvelous dinner. "They told me I could spend the night in their barn," Hoskins said. "I lay down on a bale of hay and fell asleep, quite exhausted. A few minutes later, or so it seemed, I was woken with a start by someone shaking me and screaming at me in German.

"I opened my eyes to find a young man leaning over me and I said something like 'Good grief! What's going on?' He smiled suddenly and said in English 'Relax. Come with me!' "

Hoskins had finally been collected by the Comet Line. Had he been shocked into responding in German to the rude awakening, his contact would have assumed that he was a German intelligence agent trying to infiltrate the line and undoubtedly would have killed him on the spot.

Hoskins was first taken to a Carmelite monastery in Namur, where he was hidden for three weeks while false papers were made out for him. During those weeks, said Hoskins, "I was rehearsed over and over again on how to respond when asked to show my work permit, travel papers and identity card. I was repeatedly tested on my cover story—I was supposed to be a Flemish commercial traveller going to Biarritz to sell bathroom ceramics. Tell-tale British habits like whistling or standing with my hands in my pockets were drummed out of me. I was taught how to behave in safe houses—to stay away from windows, to walk about without shoes, and to avoid flushing the lavatory too often.

Andrée "Dédée" de Jongh, the mastermind of the Belgian-based Comet escape line, dyed her fair hair black to prevent identification. Dédée was inspired to start the line by childhood heroine Edith Cavell, an English-born nurse in Belgium who had been shot by the Germans in the First World War for helping 600 Allied soldiers to escape to Holland.

I was told how to follow the guides, to walk on the other side of the street, to travel in different compartments in a train, or opposite ends of a bus."

Toward the end of his stay, Hoskins was introduced to Dédée, who gave him his final briefing. "It was very detailed. At Bressels, for example, the guides were going to be switched. My first guide would go to the station bookstall, buy a paper and hand it to someone else. I was to follow that person to a church, where I was to sit in the third pew from the front on the right hand side and wait for a man with the Belgian national colors in a little *boutonnière*. When he left, I was to follow him out and he would lead me to a safe house where I was to spend the night. The organization was absolutely extraordinary. Since I was not a Roman Catholic, I was even told how to bless myself with holy water and how to genuflect in the church."

Dressed in a charcoal-gray suit and a black Homburg and carrying an attaché case with his ceramic samples, Hoskins linked up in Brussels with two crew members from his Wellington, both of whom had also been collected by the Comet Line. Then, escorted by Dédée, the three of them traveled to Paris without incident. While changing trains at Lille, they spotted three men on another platform dressed in a similar fashion and looking, to Hoskins' eyes, very much like RAF evaders. (A few weeks later, they would see the same three men on a beach at a small French town near the Spanish border—but the two groups never joined forces.)

In Paris, Hoskins and his crewmen were put up in a safe house while waiting for Dédée to arrange to take them farther south. Meanwhile, they thoroughly enjoyed themselves. They queued up with German soldiers to see Napoleon's tomb, visited music halls and traveled on crowded metro trains shoulder to shoulder with the Wehrmacht.

After three weeks in Paris, they moved on—again by train—first to Biarritz and then to Saint-Jean-de-Luz, in the foothills of the Pyrenees. A 16-year-old girl led them from the station to a safe house, where they were disguised as Basque peasants in berets and denim working clothes and rope-soled sandals.

"We were not there long," Hoskins remembered, "before we were told that the great day had come. We cycled up to a farm in the foothills where we met Dédée and Florentino, a Basque smuggler who guided RAF evaders across the frontier. As soon as it was dark, we set off on foot, each of us with a pack on our backs. We crossed the frontier between two blockhouses and could hear the Spanish frontier guards having a party in one blockhouse.

"Florentino kept going at a murderous pace and we began to fall further and further behind. In the end, Dédée and Florentino were carrying all our packs. She was very annoyed that we simply could not keep up; she was only a slip of a girl, but she had enormous strength and courage. Finally, when we could go no further, she told us to hide in a ditch at the side of the road while she and Florentino went on into San Sebastián to get transport. We were so tired we were happy to agree and the three of us jumped into the ditch and fell asleep. We were later awakened by the sound of car doors slamming—Dédée had come back by taxi to pick us up!"

After reaching San Sebastián, Hoskins was picked up by Creswell of MI 9 and routed through Madrid to Gibraltar, where he boarded a plane for England. He was home in time for Christmas, 1942.

By the end of 1942, the Comet Line had extended its operations from Belgium into Holland and Luxembourg, and O'Leary had stretched his network into Normandy, across the Belgian border, through central France, and along the Swiss and Italian borders toward the Mediterranean coast. On the nights when Allied bombers bound for Germany passed over Holland, Belgium and northern France, escape-line scouts went out to look for injured crash victims, aimless wanderers or airmen already hidden by local patrols. Once collected and fitted out with civilian clothes and counterfeit papers, the airmen were escorted, usually by young women (who were much less likely to be stopped for questioning), along the escape line's chain of safe houses.

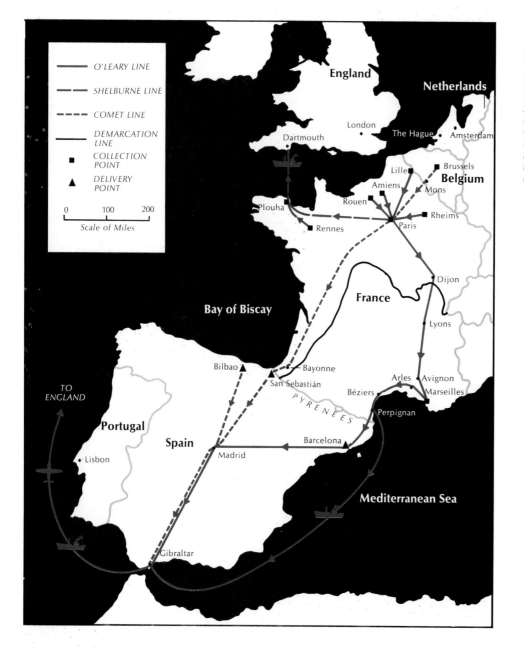

Three main escape routes were used by underground workers to rescue downed Allied airmen and other fugitives from Europe. The O'Leary and Comet Lines collected the fugitives at scattered points (squares) and, avoiding the heavy concentration of Germans guarding the Atlantic coast, sent them by train to the south of France. Some were evacuated by boat to British Gibraltar; however, most reached Gibraltar via the Pyrenees, aided by officials from British consulates (triangles). After intensive Allied air raids disrupted French train travel in 1944, the Shelburne Line was set up to bring out airmen by sea from Brittany.

Dressed in civilian clothes, three downed Allied airmen and their French guide enjoy a leisurely stroll among German soldiers in Paris in 1943. They had been rescued by an escape line and were awaiting the next stage of their journey to England via Spain. A Pathé News cameraman who belonged to the escape group filmed the brazen tour, including one richly satisfying moment when a German soldier lighted an airman's cigarette.

The most efficient escape lines installed elaborate security systems, called "cut-outs," all down their length. The cut-outs were designed to isolate each section of the line, so that only one link could be betrayed or "blown" by any German penetration. As bomber pilot Hoskins had learned, a guide from one section of the line would lead an Allied airman to a public place, such as a park or church, and then leave him. About 15 minutes later, a guide from the next section of the line would arrive and, after exchanging a prearranged password with the airman, would lead him to the next rendezvous. The two guides would be unknown to each other. They made contact by public telephone in code or by prearranged signals: a geranium plant in a shop window, for example, meant that it was safe for the guide to pick up an evader at a certain park bench; if the plant was removed, the guide knew that the Gestapo was in the area or perhaps had the pickup point under surveillance. Even a guide who was arrested and tortured could not betray the unknown next guide.

The safe houses where evaders stayed overnight were chosen with great care. Usually owned by elderly couples without inquisitive children, they had two exits, thick curtains and neighbors who were not too nosy. As a rule, the owners were not only trustworthy but also cool, skillful and well organized; they led perfectly normal lives, never betraying—by so much as an unusually large purchase of food—that they had visitors. Above all, they were courageous. If a safe house was blown, the evaders could claim prisoner-of-war status under the Geneva Convention, but their hosts could expect only the most brutal treatment, and almost certain death, at the hands of the Germans.

In spite of the tight security measures, both the Comet and O'Leary Lines were eventually penetrated by German agents. In part, the lines fell victim to their very success:

they kept growing until by 1943 their size had become a liability, making it impossible for a single leader to maintain control effectively. As more and more new helpers were enlisted, the danger of betrayal or a careless mistake increased proportionately.

The O'Leary Line was betrayed by a veteran British escape worker, Harold Cole. Cole had been a fearless and trusted courier in the early days of the line; his friends believed him to be an Army captain who had been stranded at Dunkirk. In fact, he was a sergeant who had deserted before Dunkirk, taking with him the funds of the sergeants' mess, and who had a long record of civilian convictions for housebreaking and fraud. None of this came to light until much later, but in September 1941 O'Leary had become suspicious when the smooth-talking Cole was seen with his mistress at a Marseilles party when he was supposed to have been in the north of France on escape-line business.

Not long afterward, O'Leary discovered that money Cole was supposed to pass on to an agent in Lille had never arrived. Cole was summoned to a meeting of the escape-line leaders in Marseilles and accused of stealing the money. He vehemently denied the accusation until the agent

who was supposed to have received it was called in from a back room. At this, Cole broke down and confessed. He was shut in a bathroom while the group debated what action to take; at least one leader argued for killing him on the spot. Before a decision could be made, a sound was heard from the bathroom and the leaders discovered that Cole had escaped through the window.

Soon afterward the Abbé Carpentier was arrested and clapped in prison. He smuggled out a message saying Cole had given the Gestapo a 30-page typed statement that listed the name and address of every resistance worker known to him. By then many others were being arrested. About 50 members of the O'Leary Line were executed.

In spite of these losses, the O'Leary Line carried out its most spectacular operation after Cole's treachery. Toward the end of 1942, O'Leary heard that his old Scots comrade Ian Garrow was to be sent from a French concentration camp to the death camp at Dachau. O'Leary, whose own escape from prison had been engineered by Garrow, was determined to repay the debt.

Mauzac, the concentration camp in the Dordogne where Garrow was held, was surrounded by three rings of barbed

A crowded British landing craft prepares to leave Norway's Lofoten Islands after a successful Commando raid in 1941. The Commandos destroyed 18 factories that made glycerin for German explosive manufacturers. And they brought back 315 Norwegian recruits: The men volunteered to fight for the Allies, and eight women joined the Norwegian Red Cross.

Norwegian author Sigrid Undset, winner of the Nobel Prize for literature in 1928, fled from the German invaders in 1940 because she feared punishment for her anti-Nazi writings. She headed northward from Oslo, choosing her route day by day and traveling by train, car, boat and on foot. Her circuitous 1,200-mile journey finally ended more than a month later in neutral Stockholm, only 265 miles east of her original point of departure in Oslo.

wire and was very heavily guarded. Garrow's only chance, O'Leary concluded, was to dress in the uniform of one of the French soldiers guarding the camp and walk out with them when they went off duty. O'Leary made contact with a susceptible guard and offered him a bribe of 216,000 francs—about six years' salary—if he would smuggle a uniform into the camp. Having received the man's agreement and turned over about half of the money, O'Leary then hurried to Toulouse and set tailor Paul Ulmann to work making a uniform to fit Garrow. Within two days the uniform was ready, and O'Leary rushed it back to Mauzac on November 30, 1942. He was stunned to discover that Mauzac was no longer guarded by soldiers, but by gendarmes—a result of the German occupation of Vichy 19 days earlier and the subsequent demobilization of Vichy's army. The uniform O'Leary had brought was now useless.

After the initial shock, it occurred to O'Leary that the change of guards might actually be to his advantage: the newly assigned gendarmes were unlikely to know each other by sight. So O'Leary hastened back to Ulmann and ordered a new uniform. The weary tailor and his wife finished it 48 hours later.

At 6:45 a.m. on December 6, 1942, Ian Garrow walked out of Mauzac dressed as a French gendarme and immediately disappeared down the O'Leary Line. O'Leary traveled with Garrow as far as the Spanish border.

During the early months of 1943, the O'Leary Line was again infiltrated by a traitor, and many agents working in the north of France, including Louis Nouveau, were rounded up by the Gestapo. On March 2, O'Leary arranged to meet with an agent named Roger Le Neveu from Paris to get a firsthand report on what had happened. The rendezvous was a café in Toulouse.

When O'Leary arrived at the café, Le Neveu was waiting for him. O'Leary sat down and said, "Tell me quickly, do you know who has been giving us away in Paris?"

"Yes," Le Neveu replied with a grin, "I know him very well." O'Leary felt the muzzle of a revolver press into his neck, and a voice behind him said, "Don't move."

O'Leary's arrest completed a double tragedy. Only six weeks earlier, German agents had raided a farm in the foothills of the Pyrenees that served as the starting point for the Comet Line's trek across the Spanish border. Dédée and three RAF evaders were arrested. Although she admitted

being the leader of the Comet Line, the Gestapo refused to believe that a mere girl could be in control of such a large and complex organization. Dédée spent the remainder of the War in the Ravensbrück concentration camp. O'Leary was sent to Dachau, but he too survived.

The arrest of both Dédée and O'Leary proved to be less of a disaster to the escape programs than MI 9 had feared. To be sure, the O'Leary Line never did fully recover from its double dose of treachery; but Françoise Dissart in Toulouse somehow managed to continue dispatching small parties of evaders to Spain right up to France's liberation in 1944. The Comet Line survived the loss of Dédée and numerous other agents; friends stepped forward to continue Dédée's work, and they kept the line functioning until the Allies landed in Normandy. Indeed, the number of evaders leaving France in 1943 actually increased as numerous smaller lines took up the slack left by the collapse of O'Leary's organization. By the end of the year, at least nine separate lines were sending airmen to Spain on the average of three a day.

Despite the steady traffic of escapers and evaders, the overland route through France was becoming increasingly difficult as sabotage teams and Allied bombing spread havoc through the French railroad system in preparation for the D-Day invasion. By early 1944, reports began reaching London that large numbers of airmen were holed up in châteaus and on farms along France's northwestern coast, unable to make their way south to Spain.

To repatriate this imperiled accumulation of valuable airmen, MI 9 planned a daring and complex series of sea evacuations that required close cooperation between the Royal Navy and a group of patriotic fishermen based around the village of Plouha, on the north coast of Brittany.

The new escape line devised for this operation was codenamed Shelburne and was commanded by Sergeant Major Lucien Dumais, a Canadian Commando who had escaped to the south of France after the great raid on Dieppe in 1942. The O'Leary organization had spirited him out of France. Now an agent for MI 9, Dumais and a radio operator had returned to France in October 1943 to begin planning for Shelburne.

Their efforts bore first fruit on the night of January 29, 1944. Nineteen men—13 American and four RAF fliers and two French volunteers for the Allied armed forces—were picked up from a small and secluded beach near Plouha in a precisely executed evacuation that served as a model for four others during the following two months. The five Shelburne evacuations returned a total of 118 airmen to England and constituted the last major escape operation before Allied armies rolled ashore in Normandy in June.

All told, the dozen or more escape lines in Western Europe between 1940 and 1944 had returned several hundred soldiers and an estimated 3,000 Allied airmen. For this contribution to the Allied war effort, the escape workers paid a high price. The official records of MI 9 listed the names of some 500 courageous civilians who died for their participation in escape lines. According to James Langley of MI 9, hundreds of other escape-line workers unconnected with his organization disappeared without a trace in Gestapo prisons and German death camps. Langley estimated that one escape-line worker lost his life for every fighting man who was led to safety.

A French couple pass a convivial evening in a London club founded early in the War as a place where escapees could get together with fellow countrymen. The rendezvous, called Le Petit Club Français, was established in a basement by a Welsh woman sympathetic to the French.

GERMAN COUNTERMEASURES

A French resistant smiles mockingly as a German firing squad takes aim at him. The soldiers positioned the victim at the corner of a building to avoid ricochets.

CLAMPING DOWN ON THE RESISTANCE

At the start of the Occupation, the Germans scrupulously followed Adolf Hitler's rule of thumb: "A clever conqueror will always if possible impose his demands on the conquered by installments." The invaders initially made a point of avoiding confrontations with the local citizens and settled for fines instead of taking tough punitive action. In fact, little more than a nighttime curfew limited the daily activities of most citizens.

But the control measures imposed by the Germans were far from lax. Throughout the occupied countries of Western Europe, adult males were forced to carry as many as half a dozen different forms of identification: standard identity card with a photograph and sometimes a thumbprint, work permit, ration card, military service discharge, medical certificate of exemption from forced labor, and a special permit for travel near a frontier or coast. These papers could be demanded at any time by the Abwehr (military intelligence), the SS, the Gestapo or any of a variety of other German security organizations. There were 69 Abwehr offices and 131 Gestapo stations in France alone.

Besides harassing the underground themselves, the Germans deputized the Milice and a number of other French auxiliaries to assist them in keeping order and pursuing resistants. "There are more than 360 types of cheese in France," said a Gestapo official. "Our French agents will be more varied than the French cheeses!"

Enraged by the increasing violence of the Resistance, all of these forces responded in kind. They put to death as many as 50 Frenchmen for each assassination by the underground, and, with the aid of torture-induced confessions or denunciations by undercover Miliciens, they shattered many Resistance networks. It is estimated that the Germans executed some 25,000 Frenchmen and deported another 200,000 to concentration camps, where perhaps half of them perished. Yet even as the death rate spiraled, the Resistance reacted with still more violence. Threatened one underground newspaper: "For an eye, both your eyes and for a tooth, your whole mouthful!"

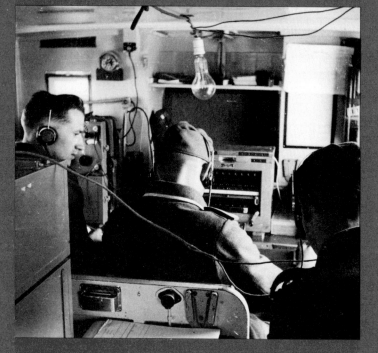

Funkspiel (Radio game) Gestapo members use an array of direction-finding equipment in a van to track down a transmitter used by the Resistance.

German border guards examine a railroad passenger's identity papers and travel permit at the demarcation line between occupied and unoccupied France.

German troops in a flat-bottomed boat launch a search through the labyrinthine sewer system under Paris in 1944, looking for Resistance workers on the run.

MANHUNTS, ARRESTS AND IMPRISONMENT

German Occupation forces pressed their pursuit of resistants on the sea as well as on land. They ransacked fishing boats entering and leaving ports of the occupied nations to catch any Resistance messengers trying to slip into or out of the coun-try. And to reinforce their elaborate net of checkpoints along coasts, borders and key transport routes, the Germans periodically staged what they called "rat hunts"—great sweeps through the villages and rugged hinterlands of central and southern France, where large numbers of young Frenchmen had sought refuge from forced labor in Germany and were forming the Resistance bands called maquis.

As the number of arrests multiplied, the prisons became filled with underground fighters and innocent suspects alike, all of whom slowly withered on a diet that seldom exceeded 600 calories a day. "If they took the bugs out of the soup, we would all starve to death, and dry up and blow out the window," one inmate wrote on the wall of his cell at the notorious Fresnes prison just south of Paris.

Troops patrol the forbidding Glières region of southeastern France, where militant resistants of a large maquis were hiding in primitive mountain camps.

Wearing full battle gear for an inspection, seagoing German police bear down on a French fishing boat as it chugs out of the Channel port of Le Havre in 1941.

Hunting resistants in a wild section of France, one German soldier holds a gun on a suspect as another checks a map of the area. The Germans may have used

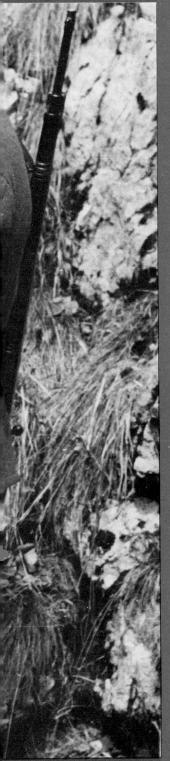

Members of a roving German patrol guard fugitives caught trying to sneak across the border into unoccupied France.

this photograph for propaganda.

Resistants who have just been brought in to a German prison in France face the walls and wait for interrogation.

Handprints on a wall (above) are mute testament to the anguish caused by electric torture inflicted by the Gestapo. Victims, hung from the electric contacts at bottom left, clutched at the wall's padded surface, which was kept wet to improve the electrical contact.

PLAIN AND FANCY GESTAPO TORTURES

When German security police arrested suspected resistants and foreign agents, they assumed their captives knew vital secrets about the underground. If threats failed, the Germans applied torture to make their prisoners cooperate. They often flailed victims with truncheons, but this rudimentary technique had to be employed with caution; torturers who were carried away by enthusiasm sometimes beat a captive so severely that he died of internal injuries before he talked.

In the four-story Gestapo headquarters at No. 93 Rue Lauriston in Paris, more refined methods were employed, including immersing the captives in enormous tubs of ice water until they were half-frozen and nearly drowned, lashing them in painful positions, dislocating their joints and —one of the most effective treatments of all—racking them with high-voltage electrical shocks.

Gestapo men in their headquarters in Paris used this thumbscrew to break the finger joints of their victims and extort their secrets.

A Resistance agent, lashed hand and foot to a wooden beam, hangs between two chairs in a German torture chamber. This photograph was made by his Gestapo torturers, who took professional interest in improving their skills.

Only rubble remains of the stone houses of Vassieux on France's Vercors Plateau after the Germans systematically destroyed the town in retaliation for local

resistance. First Luftwaffe fighter-bombers plastered Vassieux. Then Wehrmacht troops moved in and burned many buildings with villagers locked inside.

5

At one time or another, innumerable people in the German-occupied countries of Western Europe glimpsed the same horrifying scene. "I saw a train pass," wrote a Frenchwoman named Edith Thomas in 1942. "In front, a car containing French police and German soldiers. Then came cattle cars, sealed. The thin arms of children clasped the grating. A hand waved outside like a leaf in a storm. When the train slowed down, voices called 'Mama.' And nothing answered except the squeaking of the springs. The truth: stars worn on breasts, children torn from their mothers, men shot every day, the methodical degradation of an entire people. The truth is censored. We must cry it from the rooftops."

Few people—not even Edith Thomas—could know the full truth. According to the Germans, the cattle cars were transporting Jewish men, women and children to local internment camps. In fact, the Jews were ultimately destined for nightmare camps in Poland—Auschwitz, Belzec, Chelmno, Lublin, Sobidor and Treblinka—where they would be systematically exterminated.

Even if the Nazis' aim of genocide was unknown or only suspected, everyone was aware that the Jews had been singled out for special persecution, beginning with their wholesale arrest and deportation. Many of the people who saw trains or trucks carrying them away privately pitied the victims and were sickened by the Nazis' actions—but to attempt to protect the Jews involved risks that most of them were unwilling to take. Other people—anti-Semites, conformists and simple opportunists—cooperated with the Germans in rounding up their Jewish countrymen. Yet tens of thousands of citizens were moved by compassion, religious belief or moral conviction to resist the Occupation and aid the Jews. Regardless of the dangers, they hid Jews in their homes, forged papers to give them lifesaving new identities and smuggled them to safety in neutral countries. Their perilous labors as their brothers' keepers helped to save at least a quarter million Jews from certain death.

In France, efforts to protect the Jews were shaped by the divided status of the country: The occupied and unoccupied zones instituted different anti-Semitic measures and enforced them with different degrees of effectiveness.

Well before the Germans started to pressure officials in the unoccupied zone to enact anti-Semitic legislation,

THEIR BROTHERS' KEEPERS

the Vichy government—bargaining for favorable armistice terms and political concessions—bowed to Nazi creed by reducing the Jews to inferior citizenship. Jews were banned from any public office or government post that could influence cultural life. The proportion of Jews admitted to universities and the professions was strictly limited. A General Commission for Jewish Questions was set up to register Jews and to isolate them from the non-Jewish population.

The Vichy government made a clear distinction between French-born and foreign-born Jews, many of whom were refugees from prewar persecution in Germany, Austria and eastern Europe. French Jews could claim exemption from anti-Semitic measures if they had won military decorations, had made important civic contributions or belonged to a family that had resided in France for at least five generations. No such possibilities existed for foreign-born Jews. A Vichy decree in October 1940 authorized their internment. About 7,500 German and Austrian Jews whom the Germans had transported over the border into France were immediately sent to camps in the Pyrenees. Eight hundred of them died of starvation, cold and disease in the winter of 1940-1941. That was just the beginning.

In the occupied zone, the Germans introduced their first anti-Semitic measures in September 1940. After defining Jews in racial terms (anyone with two Jewish grandparents was considered Jewish) and ordering a census of the Jewish community, the conquerors decreed that any business with a Jewish manager or owner had to display a bilingual sign bearing the words *"Jüdisches Geschäft"* and *"Entreprise juive"*—"Jewish business"—in black letters on a yellow background. At first, the Parisians considered the order absurd and enjoyed making jokes about it. One popular story told of a beautiful prostitute in the Champs-Elysées who, when propositioned by a German officer, snarled at him *"Entreprise juive"* and stalked off.

By spring 1941, the jokes no longer seemed funny. In May, French police ordered 3,600 foreign-born Jews in Paris to report to a sports stadium. They were arrested and sent to an internment camp at Beaune-la-Rolande, in north-central France. More roundups followed; within a year, 30,000 Jews were interned in camps in the occupied zone.

May of 1942 brought the first systematic deportations of foreign-born Jews from French internment camps in the occupied zone to the death camps in the east. According to country-by-country quotas set up by German SS Chief Heinrich Himmler as part of what the Nazis secretly called the "final solution to the Jewish problem," France was to send 100,000 Jews to Auschwitz within the next three months.

Himmler's requirements set in motion a massive roundup of Jews who were still at liberty. On the night of July 16, 1942, some 9,000 French policemen fanned out through the darkened streets of Paris to arrest Jews whose names and addresses they had culled from files assembled during a Jewish census a few months before. Many of the victims had been warned, by notes pushed through their mailboxes, or by anonymous telephone calls, that the *grande rafle*—the big roundup—was about to happen. Some went into hiding. A few took their own lives.

Exactly 12,884 Jews were arrested that night. Of that total, fewer than 400 would one day return from the concentration camps; of the 4,051 children, none survived.

The July 16 roundup marked the real beginning of underground activity in behalf of the Jews. Most of the early recruits were Jewish themselves: young refugees from central and eastern Europe. Many of them had been members of the Communist Party or other radical organizations in their own countries and were experienced in clandestine activities. And since they were earmarked for immediate deportation, they fought fiercely.

In both the occupied and unoccupied zones, they took part in the full range of underground activities, manufacturing explosives, sabotaging German installations, assassinating Germans and collaborators, forging identity papers or food ration cards, gathering intelligence for transmission to London. But their top priority was the desperate battle to help their fellow Jews slip through the Nazi net. The children were easier than adults to spirit away from internment camps; even a hard-boiled camp guard would occasionally look the other way to permit the escape of a small child. And sympathetic peasant families found it easy to absorb another youngster or two into their homes.

Jewish women as well as men played an active role in the groups of resistants. The women, less likely to incur suspicion, were messengers, gunrunners and couriers for false documents. At a secret document plant at the University of Grenoble, so many female agents came to collect forged papers that the chief of the operation—a student—was suspected by his professors of womanizing instead of working.

Gradually, the foreign Jews were joined in the Resistance activities by French-born Jews, some of them members of two veteran Jewish welfare groups, one a children's aid agency, the other a workers' organization. At the beginning of the Occupation, these and other groups like them had been authorized by Vichy to organize aid to the Jewish refugees in internment camps. Not yet realizing the full implications of the Nazis' anti-Semitic policies, and naïvely assuming that the camps were only temporary placement centers for impoverished foreign Jews, some Jewish welfare workers organized classes in the trades and crafts with an eye toward training the incarcerated Jews for future employment. But after the deportations to the east began, it became apparent that no Jews were to be freed. And when the Germans extended their occupation to the entire country in November of 1942, the French-born Jews were hunted down as well. As their leaders pondered the purpose of the arrests and deportations, they grew ever more fearful. A few leaped to the right conclusion. Georges Loinger, a worker in the children's aid group who attended a top-level meeting

Rabbi Marcus Melchior, who warned the members of his Copenhagen synagogue that the Germans intended to round up Denmark's Jews, owed his own escape to a Christian friend. The rabbi and his family were hidden for eight days in the home of a Lutheran pastor who arranged to have them smuggled to neutral Sweden on board a Danish fishing boat.

in Lyons, later reported that Joseph Weill, the organization's president, "told us brutally that there was no point in deceiving ourselves. We were facing a genocide. Anyone taken by the Germans was dead."

Thereafter, Weill's organization toiled skillfully and tenaciously to smuggle Jews out of France. Worker Georges Garel organized an elaborate children's rescue network that became known as the Garel Circuit. The clandestine centers he set up throughout France received children who had been spirited out of camps or were brought in by parents before the police arrived for the expected arrest. The circuit operated under the aegis of Archbishop Saliège of Toulouse, who located Catholic homes for many children and placed convents at Garel's disposal for hiding others. Other children—sometimes entire families—were smuggled from convent to convent en route to neutral Switzerland.

Loinger, charged with organizing escape routes, set up an ingenious means of crossing the Swiss border at Annemasse, opposite Geneva in the Haute-Savoie region. The front for this operation was a holiday camp for the children of railway employees, and all of the Jewish children who arrived there were represented as campers, with Loinger posing as their physical-education instructor. "There was a football field just on the border," he recalled years later. "I led football teams there for matches. At the end of each match, the number of players was smaller. We would go home and then come back to play another match and so on, until all of the kids had been passed to Switzerland.

"The mayor of Annemasse pretended to be a collaborationist, but was actually a resistant and knew all about my doings. But after a while the Germans also learned about them, so it became dangerous for me to make the actual crossings. I had to ask the help of professional 'passeurs.' Of course we had to pay them a certain amount for each child. To get the money, I used to cross the border and go to Switzerland to collect it. I dressed as a cyclist with a racing bike and hid the money—two or three million francs, a lot of money at the time—in the extra tire."

The money that Loinger collected in Switzerland for the organization to aid children was provided by the so-called Joint (the American Joint Distribution Committee) and was donated primarily by Jews in the United States. The committee contributed funds to any group that was willing to give help to the Jews, including non-Jewish organizations.

One non-Jewish beneficiary of the Joint was the dynamic Christian Friendship organization, which worked closely with Weill's children's group. It was founded in 1942, ostensibly to find food and clothing for indigent foreigners. It did those things—but it also rescued Jewish families from internment and located homes where they hid until escape was possible. One of the group's founders was a Jesuit priest from Lyons, Father Pierre Chaillet, who also wrote tracts for the underground press under the pseudonym Testis. His writings stressed the fundamental antipathy between Christianity and Nazism and aimed at pushing Catholics into active Resistance work in behalf of Jews.

The Christian Friendship organization grew steadily in spite of a series of reverses. In the fall of 1942, Father Chaillet was arrested for refusing to surrender 50 Jewish children to Vichy authorities. He escaped from prison four months later, only to discover that the Gestapo had arrested many of his workers and closed several of his offices. Nevertheless, he resumed his work. A marked man, he was apprehended again but escaped imprisonment by eating his identity card. By the end of the Occupation, Father Chaillet and his workers had saved hundreds of Jewish children.

Ultimately, dozens of Resistance groups operated chiefly to save the Jews of France. Some of them shared facilities and escape routes and coordinated their activities closely. Thanks largely to their dedication and cooperation, about 200,000 of France's 300,000 Jews survived.

Unlike France, Holland had few good hiding places for Jews. It had no mountains, no woodlands to speak of, no sparsely settled regions, no shared border with a neutral country. Yet with the help of the Dutch Resistance and the cooperation of a resolutely patriotic population, thousands of Jews and other fugitives disappeared into the folds of Dutch society during the German Occupation. The Dutch called the fugitives "divers" because they were compelled to dive beneath the surface of the society, hiding in attics, barns, cellars, cowsheds and back rooms all across Holland.

Some 140,000 Jews resided in Holland at the time of the German conquest in the spring of 1940; most were members of old families that had comfortably participated in Holland's political, cultural and social life for centuries.

The Germans lost no time in attacking their position. In the autumn, the occupiers instituted their first anti-Semitic measures, ordering the registration of all businesses owned by Jews and defining Jews in racial terms. In November, Jewish professors at the Universities of Leiden and Delft were dismissed; the move immediately triggered a strike by non-Jewish students at both universities, which were subsequently closed. Further restrictions against the Jews followed. They were forbidden to use public transport, enter public libraries or visit theaters and cinemas. Each new measure was greeted with protests from the non-Jews and a general rise in anti-German sentiment.

Hanns Albin Rauter, the fanatical boss of the Gestapo in the Netherlands, was enraged at the attitude of the Dutch people and gave members of the small but noisy Dutch Nazi Party free rein to deal with the Jews as they wished. Early in 1941, local Nazi thugs responded by beating up Jews at random. This provoked the first of several full-scale riots in Amsterdam and the outlying towns.

By 1942, the Germans' anti-Semitic program was in full gear. Jews were methodically registered and increasingly segregated from the non-Jewish population, and in July, the Occupation authorities began carrying out Himmler's de-

portation orders. Many of the non-Jews who had joined mass protests now concluded that they could do nothing to halt the grim exodus; German decrees made it quite clear that anyone caught helping Jews to escape would be condemned to share the Jews' fate. Yet thousands of ordinary Dutch citizens decided to run the risk.

One of these was Johannes Bogaard, a farmer at Nieuw-Vennep, not far from Amsterdam. When Bogaard learned that the deportations had begun, he went to Amsterdam and offered the only Jewish family he knew a haven on his farm. They were quick to accept and gave Bogaard a list of other Jews and their addresses. Soon scores of Jews were hiding in crude huts and dugouts on Bogaard's farm and on the neighboring farms of his father and his brother.

Bogaard took families until he could accommodate no more. Then Jewish parents begged him to find homes for their children only. Years later, he said: "Can you imagine what that meant to the parents, to give their children to someone they had never seen, whom they knew nothing about, not even his name? I had one family with seven children. Their grief was worse, much worse, than all the danger I ran."

Bogaard took some children himself, and placed others with neighbors. In many cases, he personally assisted in smuggling the youngsters out of Amsterdam. "I had to take a little girl about four years old, take this only child away from her mother. The same day I got another child about two years old and she was deaf and dumb. In the bus, when we were on the way, you couldn't say one word to comfort this younger child. She sat sobbing softly, the tears streaming down her cheeks, and the other little girl came with a handkerchief—she was crying too, because she understood very well that it wasn't as much fun to be going along as she had thought at first—and she dried the child's tears. By then, nearly everybody on the bus was crying."

But all too few farmers in the Nieuw-Vennep area were prepared to help. When Bogaard called on a neighbor who had a large farm and asked if he could place a Jewish child with him, just for a few days, the response was typical: "I wouldn't risk my family for a million guilders." Others gave much the same answer. "Because of this attitude," Bogaard said, "we got too many people ourselves. My father—with two of my brothers, one sister and my daughter to help

Danish fishermen (foreground) ferry a boatload of Jewish fugitives across a narrow sound to neutral Sweden. Within just a few weeks of the first arrests by the Germans in 1943, some 7,000 Danish Jews managed to make their way to safety on fishing boats that plied this route.

out—then had sixty-nine people on his farm; my other brother had thirteen; and I, too, had thirteen permanent ones, but there were always more."

For the fugitives themselves, hiding was a terrible ordeal. Theo Philip van Raalte and his wife found a place to hide on a farm not far from the German border, and before long they were living in a very small room with eight others. "The worst thing about the whole situation," wrote Raalte, "was that we became constant objects of pity and concern. We couldn't join in, couldn't contribute in any way. There was just one thing we could do—stay alive."

Another couple, hidden in an unheated nook under the tiled roof of a farmhouse in east Gelderland, counted the days of the ordeal, which only made each one worse. After a few weeks, the woman entered in her diary: "This is the thirty-eighth day of our hiding; I so hope there won't be thirty-eight more." There were 933 more.

The Dutch resistants who hid Jews found their resources taxed even more severely after the Germans instituted a labor draft in mid-1943. Thousands of Dutch workers refused to report and went underground. To meet the ever-increasing demand for hiding places and false papers, the National Organization for Help to People in Hiding was founded by two remarkable patriots. One was Mrs. Helena Theodora Kuipers-Rietberg, a housewife and mother of five children. The other was Pastor Frits Slomp, a Calvinist minister who had been forced to leave his pulpit in a village near the German border because of his anti-Nazi preaching.

The two met in another border town after Pastor Slomp had secretly preached in the local Reformed church. Slomp later recalled: "She said to me, 'Frits, I'm at a loss. Our boys have to go to Germany, and we simply can't permit it. I've already found places for the boys here and there, and I've hidden some Jews, but I've reached the point where I just don't know how to go on. Frits, we have to found an organization so we can give these people places to hide. Now, I thought you should do it—you should travel all over the country and stir up enthusiasm for this plan.'"

Slomp replied, "I don't dare to," but that was an answer she would not accept. "She said—and I'll never forget her words—'Oh Frits, would it really be so bad to lose your life if thousands of boys could be saved?' I could say nothing more. If you had heard the way she said it, like a mother

worried about her children, about the boys, about the hundreds of Jews for whom there was no way out, you too would have kept silent."

Pastor Slomp set out to make contacts among Allied sympathizers and fellow churchmen throughout Holland. By 1944 he had set up regional committees, and his organization had more than 15,000 volunteers helping the 300,000 people who had gone into hiding.

Many of those who tried to protect the Jews paid the ultimate price. Mrs. Kuipers-Rietberg was arrested and died at the Ravensbrück concentration camp in eastern Germany. Johannes Bogaard's family saved more than 300 lives, but Bogaard's father and brother were arrested for their activities and perished in concentration camps; his son died soon after being released from one. As for Bogaard himself—who escaped only by going into hiding—after the Occupation ended, he wrote: "We have had to look not at what we lost but at what we saved. God called us to this work and He also gave us the strength for it. As Netherlanders we could not do otherwise."

In neighboring Belgium, help for the Jews came from every segment of society. Dowager Queen Elizabeth, who remained in residence with King Leopold III throughout the Occupation, interceded with German authorities in behalf of the Jews and was able to save several thousand from deportation. Cardinal Joseph-Ernest van Roey, Belgium's Chief Prelate, ordered all Catholic institutions in the country to take in Jews whenever they could. Convents, parish priests, hospitals, church schools and child welfare agencies all helped to hide Jewish families, as did a vigorous Jewish

Dutch youths forage for firewood in the ruins of an Amsterdam house whose Jewish owners had been deported. To alleviate Holland's wartime fuel shortage, Dutch citizens demolished many such houses to obtain doors, floor boards and staircases to burn in their stoves and fireplaces.

underground. Of the 65,000 Jews who were in Belgium at the start of the Occupation, 25,000 survived.

Norway was the home of only 1,800 Jews, and the Germans expected to make short work of them. In April 1940, German troops desecrated the Jewish synagogue in the seaport of Trondheim, and a month later the Occupation authorities decreed that no Jews could leave Norway. Presently, scores of Jews were arrested on trumped-up charges, and Jewish businesses were confiscated.

But from the outset, the Norwegians resisted the Germans in general and Nazi anti-Semitic policies in particular. A nationwide Resistance organization known as the Home Front quickly took shape and set up an escape network that supplied dispossessed Jews and other fugitives with food, clothing and false identity papers and helped them slip across the border into neutral Sweden.

Vidkun Quisling, the home-grown Nazi who had briefly served as Prime Minister in 1940, took charge of an ineffective collaborationist government in February 1942 and proceeded to move against the Jews in an anxious effort to ingratiate himself with Hitler. He insisted that the Norwegian public schools revise their history syllabus to bring it in line with Nazi policies, including their anti-Semitic view that Jews were plotting to rule the world through their international economic power or to seize global control through a Communist revolution. Every history teacher in Norway refused to accept the new program. Subsequently, more than 1,300 teachers were arrested, and nearly 500 of them were sent to work on docks in the arctic port of Kirkenes, near the Finnish border. But only 50 of these teachers recanted, and at the end of six months Quisling abandoned his efforts to discipline them. The teachers returned to a hero's welcome.

Trying another tack, Quisling revived a long-dead provision of the Norwegian Constitution that banned Jews and Jesuits from the country; the xenophobic article had been drafted in 1814 and rescinded in 1851. The effect of its revival was to make all Norwegian Jews illegal aliens, laying the groundwork for their eventual deportation.

Nearly 1,000 of the Norwegian Jews had escaped into Sweden before the deportations began in November of 1942. But the rest of the Jews, reassured by the solid support of their non-Jewish countrymen, lingered too long. By

THE ORDEAL OF ANNE FRANK

Anne Frank described her diary as "my friend."

In July of 1942, a 13-year-old Jewish girl named Anne Frank went into hiding in Amsterdam and began to record her experiences in a diary that would come to apotheosize the plight of all Jews persecuted by the Germans. For more than two years Anne, her parents, her sister and four other Jews never left their hiding place *(right)* in the building that housed her father's spice-importing business. They relied on trusted employees to bring food.

In her diary, Anne expressed the agony of living in endless confinement, idleness and terror. Late in 1943, she wrote: "I wander from one room to another, feeling like a songbird whose wings have been clipped and who is hurling himself in utter darkness against the bars of his cage. . . . I go and lie on the divan and sleep to make the time pass more quickly, and the stillness and the terrible fear."

Anne's worst fears came true on August 4, 1944. The Germans found the hideaway and sent the Franks and their companions to the Bergen-Belsen concentration camp, where Anne died of typhus in March 1945.

Six rooms in this building formed the hiding place.

he small bedroom that Anne shared with a Jewish dentist overlooked a quiet courtyard.

A movable bookcase concealed stairs to the refuge.

February of 1943, more than 700 of them had been arrested and sent to Auschwitz. Only 24 of them were still alive at the end of the War.

In 1943, a British newspaper ran a story about the attitude of Denmark's King Christian X toward the 8,000 Jews in his country. "If the Germans want to introduce the yellow star in Denmark," Christian was reported as saying, "I and my whole family will wear it as a sign of highest distinction." The story was apocryphal—but true in spirit. The Danes backed their Jewish countrymen without reservation.

In fact, the national outrage that was stirred by German anti-Semitism did more to fuel the Resistance in Denmark than in any other country in the occupied West.

During the first three years of occupation, German authorities, following Hitler's orders to transform Denmark into a "model protectorate," refrained from imposing the usual harsh measures against the Jews. What anti-Semitism there was drew a swift reaction from the Danes.

Thus, in December 1941, when the Germans attempted to set fire to a Copenhagen synagogue, Danish policemen stopped them—and then created an auxiliary police unit of armed Jews who were assigned to guard the building. An anti-Semitic newspaper started by the Germans had to stop publication because it could not find subscribers. Anti-Jewish films played to empty theaters. "As time went on," recalled a Danish nurse named Gethe Kisling, "we became more and more annoyed by the situation. A strong feeling of hate began to build up in most people and a desire to be allowed to do something to fight the enemy instead of just having to behave."

These signs of rebellion beneath Denmark's placid exterior were duly reported to Hitler, and he decided in Novem-ber 1942 that the time had come to bring the Danes to heel. He appointed Karl Werner Best, a former SS storm trooper, to the post of Reich plenipotentiary and sent him to Copenhagen with orders to "rule with an iron hand." A tough Army officer, Lieut. General Hermann Hanneken, was assigned command of the Occupation forces; simultaneously, Denmark's supposedly pro-German Foreign Minister, Erik Scavenius, was made Prime Minister and instructed to form a new Cabinet politically acceptable to the Reich.

In spite of his instructions to establish rigid control, Best pursued what he called a "policy of understanding" toward the Danes; he feared jeopardizing the flow of much-needed agricultural and industrial products to Germany. In March 1943, he allowed a general election to take place as scheduled (a unique event in an occupied country) and seized upon the results as proof that his policy of moderation was working. The four major political parties, all of them represented in the Scavenius Cabinet, received nearly 95 per cent of the votes—a clear indication, Best alleged, that the vast majority of the Danes favored collaboration with Germany. In fact, only the remaining 5 per cent of the votes could have been safely construed as pro-German. They were cast for Denmark's Nazi Party.

A more conclusive set of figures was being amassed by Denmark's two major Resistance groups, one of which was Communist-led. These tight-knit organizations, stirred to action by their opposition to German anti-Semitism, tormented the occupiers with sabotage operations against factories, electric power stations and railways. In February 1943, there had been 34 attacks; the number rose to 70 in March and 78 in April. Encouraged by reports of these forays, SOE in London began delivering arms and ammunition, and stepped up its BBC broadcasts urging the Danes to re-

Inside a shed in Amsterdam (left), the getaway car of Dutch resistant Liepke Scheepstra (above) is lowered into a secret underground compartment by means of a hydraulic lift. Scheepstra's network performed strong-arm work in aid of the Jews and other fugitives.

A Dutch Nazi policeman, slain by a Resistance worker, lies sprawled in the gutter of a fog-shrouded street in the city of Haarlem in 1944.

sist. The BBC kept Danes informed of German reversals in North Africa and Russia, and the news of these defeats encouraged still more people to throw in their lot with the Resistance.

By August, when 220 incidents of sabotage took place, Best was frantic. He repeatedly demanded that the Danish government restore order, but the government had lost the support of the people and could do nothing.

On August 26, Best was summoned to Berlin to account for his failures. He was berated by Foreign Minister Joachim von Ribbentrop. Best returned to Copenhagen the follow-

ing day, pale and shaken, bringing with him an ultimatum for the Danish government: a state of emergency was to be imposed immediately.

The government voted unanimously to resign rather than accept the ultimatum. In the early hours of the following morning, German troops surrounded Danish Army garrisons, interned their soldiers and occupied key installations throughout the country. Denmark awoke on August 29 to find that martial law had been declared.

Clearly the situation was getting out of hand, and Best realized that some drastic step was needed to repair his

tattered reputation at home. He sent a long telegram to Berlin suggesting that the time was right to take measures against the Jews in Denmark. The hard-liners in Berlin were delighted to oblige with the genocidal program applied elsewhere; all too long they had suffered the embarrassment of having nearly 8,000 Jews living quite freely in a country occupied by Germany.

Almost as soon as the wheels were set in motion, Best was besieged by grave doubts; he sought reassurance from his friend Georg Duckwitz, who was shipping attaché at the German embassy in Copenhagen. Duckwitz was horrified at the change in policy; persecution of the Jews, he said, would do irreparable damage to relations between Denmark and Germany. But Berlin was already pressing Best for a firm date when the "transfer" of Jews would begin. Best ordered the roundup of Jews to start at 10 o'clock on the evening of Friday, October 1. That night marked the start of Rosh Hashana, the Jewish New Year, and he was sure the Jews would be at home.

Duckwitz, who was with Best when the decision was made, had no doubts about what he should do. As soon as he left his friend, he contacted Hans Hedtoft, a leading Danish Social Democrat, and informed him of what was going to happen. As Duckwitz had intended, the news did not take long to spread.

On the morning of Thursday, September 30, 1943, Rabbi Marcus Melchior addressed the congregation in his Copenhagen synagogue: "There will be no service this morning. Instead, I have very important news to tell you. Last night I received word that tomorrow the Germans plan to raid all Jewish homes throughout Copenhagen to arrest all the Danish Jews for shipment to concentration camps. We must take action immediately. You must leave the synagogue now and contact all relatives, friends and neighbors you know who are Jewish and tell them what I have told you. You must tell them to pass the word on to everyone they know is Jewish. You must also speak to all your Christian friends and tell them to warn the Jews. You must do this

immediately, within the next few minutes, so that two or three hours from now everyone will know what is happening. By nightfall tonight, we must all be in hiding."

By nightfall, most of the Danish Jews had disappeared into the homes of non-Jewish friends and neighbors. Sympathetic strangers also volunteered to help. Mendel Katlev, a Jewish foreman in a Copenhagen leather-goods factory, left work on hearing of the roundup and caught a commuter train home. The conductor of the train, a man Katlev saw daily but had never spoken to, asked him why he was leaving work so early. Katlev told the conductor of the German plans and remarked that he had to look for a place to hide. The conductor immediately offered refuge in his own home to Katlev, his wife and his children.

Some non-Jews sought out Jewish families and offered them keys to city apartments and country cottages. When Jorgen Knudsen, a young Copenhagen ambulance driver, heard the news, he went to a telephone booth, made off with a directory and pored through it, looking for Jewish-sounding names. All day long he drove through the city, calling on Jewish families to warn them. Several families told him they had no place to hide, so he bundled them into his ambulance and took them to Bispebjerg Hospital. There they were hidden in doctors' quarters or admitted as patients and scattered through the wards.

On the night of the roundup, only 284 Jews were arrested. In the following month, the Germans managed to find and arrest scarcely 200 more. The 7,200 Jews who escaped the Nazi roundup remained safely in hiding until they could be smuggled to Sweden in fishing boats.

One of the rescuers was 20-year-old Christian Algreen-Petersen, a Danish soldier who had been arrested as a hostage and later released. "I didn't know anything about what had been going on," he later recalled, "and when I returned home after a month in an internment camp, I was amazed to find the house full of Jews. At first my father, who had been in the Resistance from the beginning, did not want me to get involved, but there was no alternative. More

Jews were arriving every day and I took over responsibility for arranging fishing boats to take them to Sweden.

"Every day I went down to the harbor to meet fishermen in a little restaurant called The Diamond. They would ask me how many people I had to go that night and we would bargain over the price. We had to pay quite high sums for each Jew because it was very dangerous for the fishermen. If they were caught by the Germans their boat was confiscated and they were left without a living. Most of them were very good, although there were some shady characters who made a lot of money out of it. When we had a lot of people to go, we had to take what we could get. Soon we were shipping twenty, thirty, fifty Jews every night."

One night Algreen-Petersen and three of his friends ran into a Gestapo trap while they were escorting refugees to a boat waiting in Copenhagen's inner harbor. As they turned into the harbor gates, they were met by a hail of machine-gun fire. One man was killed instantly; another died a few hours later from his wounds. The others fled and made good their escape, but Algreen-Petersen was shot in the back before he got far.

"The bullet pierced my lung and I fell immediately. It was a very dark night and pouring with rain. I managed to crawl up the street, across the pavement and down steps into a cellar which was used by a man selling furniture. I pulled myself onto a divan as the owner came out of a back room. He was terrified and told me to get out because the blood was spoiling his furniture! Then his son arrived, took one look at me and said 'the man's dying.' It was terrible to here those words.

"I could hardly speak, but I managed to ask them to call an ambulance. They started arguing, about what would happen if the Gestapo came and about whether they dared or dared not to call an ambulance. Strangely, the delay was lucky for me, because by the time they had made up their minds to help, the Gestapo had left the area and when the ambulance came, I was taken to a Danish hospital."

When Algreen-Petersen recovered from his wounds, he went underground, more determined than ever to continue working with the Resistance, despite its terrors. "I was scared nearly all the time, I think everyone was. The thought of being arrested and tortured was very, very frightening. It was the little things that got to you, like meeting a friend in a restaurant and becoming aware that someone sitting near-by seemed interested in our conversation. Walking the streets at night, when it was very silent, very dark, I used to imagine the Gestapo were round every corner waiting for me. I kept on the move all the time and never stayed in the same place for more than a couple of nights.

"The worst moments were at night, trying to get to sleep. Every time I heard a car in the street, I would jump out of bed to see if the Gestapo were outside. But I never considered giving up; once you are in something like that, you just cannot walk away."

The abortive German roundup turned the model protectorate into a hotbed of Resistance activity. After the deportation of the Jews, there was no looking back, no attempt at accommodation. The various Resistance groups established a central committee called the Freedom Council to coordinate their activity and divided the country into six regions, each in direct contact with London by radio. Soon, sabotage was rampant, and Resistance groups were ambushing German soldiers on patrol in the streets of Copenhagen.

Even the luckless Jews who had been captured and deported by the Germans benefited from the Danes' new fighting spirit. The Danish government persistently badgered the Germans about the Jews' whereabouts and welfare. Danish officials made trips to inspect Theresienstadt, the camp in Czechoslovakia where the Jews were held, and they sent in frequent shipments of food, clothing and medical supplies.

Fifty-one of the Jews died there of natural causes—a toll that the Danes blamed on their captivity. But Denmark was unique among the occupied countries in one respect: so far as is known not a single one of its Jews was put to death in the Nazi gas chambers.

THE DUTCH AID THEIR JEWS

Hidden away from the German police, an elderly Jewish couple in occupied Holland pass time by reading books in their cluttered refuge in a Gentile home.

HOLLAND'S CRISIS OF CONSCIENCE

On February 22 and 23 in 1941, German police swooped down on the Jewish quarter of Amsterdam, rounded up about 400 young men and shipped them off to a concentration camp. "They forcibly entered the houses under the pretext of an arms search," a Dutch Gentile wrote. "The Amsterdam policemen had to encircle the entire quarter. One policeman was nearly in tears from anger and indignation, but what could he do?"

Many infuriated non-Jews asked themselves the same question when they heard about the arrests. And when the Dutch Communist Party flooded the city with leaflets calling for a protest strike, they responded enthusiastically, with little thought for the consequences.

On February 25, Amsterdam ground to a halt. Trams disappeared from the streets, white-collar workers left their offices and public utilities were shut down. The strike held sway for two days and spread to surrounding towns. A Gentile typist wrote, "Holland has shown spontaneously that it is not to be trifled with, that it stands up for its people, whatever race they belong to."

The real crisis began after the Germans had violently crushed the strike. Dutch Gentiles realized that they had not diverted the Germans from their plans for persecution. The Jews would have to be protected day after day, month after month, year after year, and each non-Jew, no matter how compassionate he was, was forced to ask himself if he should risk his life and the lives of his family to protect strangers over the long haul. Dutch Jewish leaders *(below)* faced a different moral dilemma. The Germans offered to temper their treatment of the Jews if the leaders would cooperate in a program of pacifying and registering their people. The leaders agreed to the plan, and unwittingly betrayed some Jews to save others.

Many Gentiles sorrowfully decided that their first duty was to their families and not to the Jews. But many Dutchmen committed themselves to a life of deadly hazard, and they saved nearly 15,000 of their Jewish countrymen.

Members of the Jewish Council, established by the Germans in February of 1941 to control the Jews, assemble at the council's headquarters in Amsterdam.

During a roundup of Jews, two Germans patrol the deserted streets of a Jewish neighborhood in Amsterdam, while others conduct a house-to-house search.

A 1941 sign permitting "limited liberty of movement for Jews" stood briefly in a park in Renkum, southeast of Amsterdam.

Separated by barbed wire fro

Signposts inscribed "Street of the Jews" in German and Dutch mark the boundary of a Jewish neighborhood in Amsterdam.

heir Jewish neighbors, Gentiles pass the Weighing House, an old Amsterdam landmark. Undaunted, children (center) talk to a Jewish lad through the fence.

VAIN PROTESTS FOR THE PERSECUTED

After the February strike, the Germans instituted a succession of anti-Semitic measures meant to isolate the Dutch Gentiles from their Jewish countrymen. Jewish coworkers were fired; self-employed Jewish professionals were prevented from practicing in the Gentile community. Jews were barred from non-Jewish homes, from public transportation and from most parks and municipal buildings. In January 1942 the Germans began herding Jews from all over Holland into Amsterdam. By 1943 most of the Dutch Jews had been confined in three districts of the city.

Time and again, Dutch Gentiles protested these measures—until protest seemed utterly futile. Some people, as one Gentile wrote, "gradually got used to Jews having the worst of it." Yet opposition flared up again in May 1942, when Jews were forced to wear a yellow star bearing the word "Jood"—"Jew." Many citizens risked the Germans' wrath by wearing yellow stars of their own, imprinted not with "Jew" but with "Roman Catholic" or "Protestant" or just plain "Dutchman."

A Jew vainly tries to outrun laughing German police during a roundup in Amsterdam. On average, each raid swept about 400 Jews into the German nets.

HELPLESS WITNESSES TO DEPORTATION ROUNDUPS

In June of 1942, Dutch Gentiles feared the worst when the German authorities announced that thousands of Jews were to report for assignments as laborers in Germany. Few Jews responded to the summons, so German police began carrying out large-scale raids on the Jewish sections. Every night, the Germans dragged Jews out of their houses, shoved them into green vans and drove them to the train station. There they were crowded into railway cars bound not for work sites but for extermination camps run by the SS.

Although one German official reported with satisfaction, "The Dutch population stood by and watched the roundup with curiosity," most of the Gentiles were, in fact, horror-stricken. Some onlookers did the little they could: they pleaded with the Germans for mercy and gave the Jews food and warm clothes; then they hurried off to break the grim news to the deportees' relatives and friends.

At gunpoint, Jews raise their hands above their heads and await further orders at an assembly point.

A German policeman drives Jews into a Poland-bound train. Some Dutch engineers called in sick to avoid making the runs—but others were always found.

145

HIDING FUGITIVES AND KEEPING THE SECRET

As the German police pressed the policy of mass removal, more and more Gentiles offered to hide the remaining Jews in their homes, even though such protection rated as a grave crime against the Reich. Said one Dutch Protestant, "We knew that we simply had to help these people, and that the Lord would watch over us all."

A network of skillful amateur smugglers brought hosts and guests together—a perilous task, since Jews were not permitted to travel. The underground workers transported Jews to refuges in crates, baker's carts and even in a mourner's carriage. On occasion they donned stolen SS uniforms, handcuffed their charges and boldly paraded past German guards.

Once the Jews had reached their havens, they usually stayed indoors, tucked away in attics, cellars, closets and other nooks. But no matter how effective the concealment, it would be worthless if the Germans overheard any loose talk about their presence—or received a tip from an unfriendly neighbor. So Dutch sympathizers shared the dangerous secret with as few people as possible. In one case, a mother and her grown daughter visited each other every weekend throughout the Occupation, and neither told the other that she was hiding Jews.

On the roof of her host's house, a Jewish fugitive descends through the trap door to her hiding place.

Creeping through a secret passageway, a Jew enters his refuge inside a Dutch patriot's home.

After raising a closet's fake floor, a Jewish woman emerges from her cramped quarters. Some hide-outs had no standing room and little light or ventilation.

A Dutch farmer pauses beside a thatched hovel where he conceals Jews.

Two sons of a family named Bogaard join hands with young Jewish guest

HUMBLE HAVENS
IN THE COUNTRYSIDE

Like Holland's city folk, many farmers answered German predations against their Jewish countrymen by hiding fugitives. Often such hosts were themselves struggling to survive; the saying went around, "The poor offer you shelter, the rich someone else's address." But some Jews could pay for board, even though their assets had been confiscated; the money came from the secret National Assistance Fund, set up by non-Jewish businessmen in 1943.

The farmers hid their guests in houses, barns, chicken houses and storage huts. Since neighbors rarely lived close by, Jews could go outdoors, and many worked as farm hands to help earn their keep. But farmers and their wards always had to stay on guard. Dutch Nazis and gangs of thugs roamed the countryside in search of Jewish fugitives; each capture was rewarded by a small bounty paid out of rents and interest from confiscated Jewish properties.

All together, some 25,000 Jews went into hiding in Holland. Nearly half were eventually caught and sent to concentration camps, along with the Dutch hosts who had answered the call of conscience.

on their farm near Nieuw-Vennep, 14 miles southwest of Amsterdam. During the Occupation, the Bogaards saved more than 300 Jews, many of them children.

6

At 2 o'clock on the morning of July 4, 1943, six shadows detached themselves from the looming black silhouette of the locomotive roundhouse at Troyes, an industrial town about 100 miles southeast of Paris. The shadows flitted into the surrounding streets and vanished. A half hour passed; then a loud explosion brought the Germans belated news of the group's visit to the roundhouse. As soldiers assembled and poked around to check the damage, another blast shook the building, then another and another.

By the time the local German commander arrived on the scene, his troops had withdrawn to a safe distance. He climbed up onto the footplate of a locomotive on a siding to berate his men for their timidity, but before he was able to open his mouth, a nearby locomotive blew up. The commander sprang from the footplate like a scalded cat and raced for the safety of his waiting car. There were 13 explosions that night; six locomotives were destroyed and six more seriously damaged.

Two months later, in September 1943, three saboteurs disguised as shipyard workers boarded a German minesweeper anchored in the Seine River at Rouen, saying they had been ordered to make some last-minute adjustments before the ship sailed in the morning. The minesweeper had just passed its sea trials after a complete, expensive refit. At 11 o'clock that night, a bomb blasted a hole five feet by three feet in the ship's hull. Six minutes later, the river had swallowed up the whole minesweeper except for the top of its funnel.

On January 7, 1944, two British secret agents parachuted into southern France near the town of Figeac. They had hardly hidden their chutes when they were greeted by the foreman of the Ratier aircraft works, which was turning out variable-pitch propellers for the Luftwaffe. Together the men fashioned several bombs in a cheese shop belonging to another conspirator. Then still another member of the band, who was wearing a white chef's hat for the occasion, carried the explosives across town on a large tray covered with a fresh napkin, drawing hardly a glance from the German street patrols. He secreted the bombs in an automobile, and after dark he and his colleagues drove to the Ratier factory, where they let themselves in with keys that had been supplied by the foreman.

The town of Figeac was soon rocked by a terrific explo-

AN EPIDEMIC OF SABOTAGE

sion. A 30-ton metal press was lifted 25 feet and smashed to pieces, and several other machines that fabricated the propeller blades were destroyed. The factory produced no more propellers for the Luftwaffe.

Sabotage attacks such as these were affectionately referred to as "bangs" by those who perpetrated them, and they occurred all over German-occupied Europe in ever-increasing frequency through 1943 and early 1944. Like the escape-line workers, the saboteurs paid dearly for their successes; thousands were captured, tortured and executed by the Gestapo and the Sicherheitsdienst, the German special police force charged with eliminating resistants. But patriots in the occupied countries had perceived that the Germans, stalemated in Russia and defeated in North Africa, were not winning the War, and this encouraged more and more of them to join the various Resistance movements—and to set off ever larger and bolder bangs.

These missions of destruction were largely coordinated by the British Special Operations Executive. By laboriously planting trained agents throughout the occupied countries, SOE had fostered the growth of dozens of flourishing networks of saboteurs in France, the Netherlands, Belgium and parts of Scandinavia. The agency's headquarters in London radioed intelligence to the saboteurs, suggesting where bangs would do the enemy the most harm, and air-dropped increasingly large supplies of firearms, ammunition and, most especially, plastic explosive, the devilishly efficient cyclonite concoction that, being as pliable as putty, could be wrapped around or stuck to anything a saboteur might want to blow up.

The great advantage of sabotage over bombing was its stiletto precision. A few determined men with a dozen pounds of plastic explosive could destroy the locomotives for German troop trains or blow up the machinery in an armaments factory without harming the French, Dutch, Belgian, Danish or Norwegian civilians who lived nearby. By contrast, the heavy bombers of the RAF and the U.S. Army Air Forces often missed the vital target while plastering the surrounding homes with 500-pound bombs. French civilians, who suffered most frequently from wayward bombs, feared the Allied bombers and loathed their sledge-hammer tactics. Indeed, it was partly to protect their countrymen that the underground networks had laid plans in 1942 to expand their sabotage. In a radio message to London, the Mouvements Unis de Résistance, one of the largest networks in France, stated the case: "If you provide the explosives and indicate the targets, our groups are ready to undertake any form of demolition and extend this action; this would avoid costly and inaccurate bombing, which damages the morale of the population."

The subsequent upsurge of sabotage destroyed many targets before the bombers got to them, thus saving the lives of thousands of civilians (and, probably, hundreds of airmen). It also helped to confuse the Germans and make occupation duty a frightening and frustrating chore. Everywhere the Germans turned in 1943 and afterward, they found more and more rail lines, factories and power stations newly sabotaged into useless tangles of steel and wire.

Power stations were normal and logical targets for destruction. But in the autumn of 1942 a special, massive, complex sabotage operation was aimed at an obscure power plant in south-central Norway. To all appearances, the Norsk Hydro installation on the Hardanger Plateau had no great military importance. But Allied intelligence agencies believed that the outcome of the War might well turn on the top-secret work being done there.

The Norsk plant was the only facility in the world that was then capable of producing significant quantities of a substance known to physicists as deuterium oxide (D_2O), but generally called by the eerie name "heavy water." This experimental compound had an exotic capability: it could act as a moderator or brake on a nuclear chain reaction, absorbing fast-moving neutrons from a radioactive fuel pile of uranium. Such a brake was a prerequisite for the scientists working toward the production of an atomic bomb. Heavy water was not unique in this regard. Enrico Fermi and other physicists, who were at that very time creating the world's first self-sustaining nuclear reaction at the University of Chicago, kept their uranium fuel under control by damping it with 350 tons of graphite bricks. But all those in the forefront of atomic research knew that heavy water would do the job at least as well.

The scientists working on the Allied side were convinced that their German counterparts led the world in atomic research. So they were deeply alarmed when, in February

1942, Allied intelligence reported that the Germans had ordered the manufacture of heavy water stepped up to 10,000 pounds a year. Actually, the Germans' atomic research was aimed at harnessing nuclear energy rather than unleashing it; in particular, they hoped to use atomic power to drive submarines, reducing the frequency of dangerous refueling trips to shore bases. But only one conclusion seemed possible at the time: Hitler's Germany was racing toward the development of atomic bombs that could destroy London, obliterate all Allied forces within reach of the Luftwaffe—and win the War.

The situation appeared desperate, and a desperate remedy was concocted. A team of advance agents would parachute onto the Hardanger Plateau, near the heavily guarded hydroelectric plant. Then two large Horsa gliders carrying 34 British Commandos would be towed across the North Sea by RAF bombers and released over the plateau. The two groups would join up in late autumn, and the advance party, made up of Norwegians who knew the area, would guide the Commandos to the plant and help demolish it.

As a first step in assembling the sabotage team, SOE searched among the thousands of young Norwegians who had fled to England from their occupied homeland by boat or plane; the sifting process turned up three expert skiers from the town of Rjukan, which was less than three miles from the Norsk installation. They were Jens Poulsson, Knut Haugland and Claus Helberg. All knew the area's terrain intimately, as did the fourth member of the team, a barrel-chested plumber from Oslo named Arne Kjelstrup, who had often visited the region.

The four volunteers were sent to SOE's Scotland training base, which the Germans called the "International Gangster School." There they were taught 20 silent ways to kill an enemy soldier, plus such additional skills as fusing and detonating plastic explosive. The Norwegians were outfitted with carefully chosen winter gear, including white parkas, down-lined sleeping bags and authentic Norse cross-country skis secretly obtained from a ski shop in Iceland that sold Norwegian-made equipment. No clothing or gear of English origin would betray them in case they were stopped for interrogation.

On October 18, 1942, the four men were aboard a Halifax roaring over Norway. They heaved the coffin-sized metal boxes containing their gear and a month's rations through the plane's escape hatch. Then they dropped through the hatch themselves and hurtled past the twin-finned tail, their chutes billowing in the frosty air that signaled the approach of the early Scandinavian winter.

The Hardanger Plateau is one of the loneliest and most inhospitable places in Europe—2,500 square miles of barren rock, corrugated by fissures and ridges, dotted by frozen bogs and lakes. In winter, violent storms sweep the plateau, or freezing fog settles like a deathly blanket over its angry surface. Snow had already fallen when the four Norwegian agents landed, and it took them three days to find their equipment boxes in the drifts, and more than two weeks to trek the gear to an abandoned hunters' cabin that was within striking distance of the hydroelectric plant and near a level spot where the gliders could make a landing. Then they waited for the gliders and their cargoes of Commandos to come whooshing in.

The gliders never arrived. They had set out across the North Sea, towed by two Halifaxes, on the evening of November 19, 1942, at the start of a 400-mile journey—the longest glider tow ever attempted at that date. It ended in disaster. The first Halifax crossed the southern coast of Norway at 10,000 feet, but was unable to locate the landing site where the Norwegians were waiting. Low on fuel, the pilot turned for home but plowed into turbulence so violent that the towline parted. The glider swerved down through thick clouds and crash-landed on the top of a snow-capped mountain overlooking Lyse Fjord. Eight men were killed and four were seriously injured.

The second Halifax crossed the Norwegian coast at too low a level—the pilot was trying to fly under layers of storm cloud—and crashed into a mountain 10 miles inland. Before impact, which killed the bomber's four crewmen instantly, the pilot apparently released the towline to give the men aboard the glider a chance. The glider crash-landed on an adjoining mountainside: three men were killed and six were seriously injured.

A total of 23 Commandos survived the glider crashes. All were rounded up by the Gestapo. According to an order Hitler had issued a month before, any sabotage parties, in uniform or not, were to be "slaughtered to the last man."

The Commandos, though dressed in British uniforms, were executed as spies.

News of the disaster was radioed in stages to the four men on the Hardanger Plateau. "First," recalled Knut Haugland, the radio operator, "we got a message that the gliders had come down not too far away and we were told to search for them. Then we were asked to wait for another message and I got the sad news that both gliders had crashed. I think that was the worst moment for us all and in a strange way, it made it even more important to us that the operation should eventually succeed. We were instructed to stay in the mountains and wait for further orders." What they were not told was that they were expected to survive without supplies.

Shortly after the failure of the glider operation, the four advance agents received a message that another attacking force would be flown in—this time a small group of Norwegian volunteers. They had no idea of when the new group would arrive, but to avoid being discovered by accident in the meantime, they moved to another cabin farther from the hydroelectric plant.

By December the four men had consumed practically all of their rations, and were subsisting on a gruel made of reindeer moss—a lichen they dug from beneath the snow—and their last grains of oatmeal. By Christmastime they were starving, their sunken eyes turning yellow and red-rimmed, their bellies swollen with edema. But Poulsson, the leader, refused to give up. Day after day, he dragged himself out of his sleeping bag, put on his skis, slung a rifle over his shoulder and went hunting across the snow-clad plateau for the wilderness' only other inhabitants, reindeer. But day after day he returned to the cabin empty-handed. Appar-

In a pinpoint bombing attack coordinated by the Danish Resistance, RAF Mosquitoes obliterate the Gestapo headquarters at Aarhus University in October 1944. The raid, which freed dozens of imprisoned Danish resistants and saved the lives of countless others by destroying German files, was executed without striking a hospital that was near the target.

ently the reindeer migrations had yet to reach the plateau.

On the afternoon of the day before Christmas, Poulsson finally caught a glimpse of the first herd of the animals—about 70 of them, grazing far below him at the edge of a frozen lake. They were well out of range, but he was to leeward and knew they would not pick up his scent. Keeping behind cover as much as possible, he cautiously skied closer. But before he was able to get off a shot, the nearest animal stamped nervously and communicated its fear to the rest of the herd. Within seconds they were gone, kicking up a cloud of snow in their wake.

Poulsson soon came upon another, smaller herd. This time he removed his skis, crawled to a rock outcrop, took careful aim at a young cow reindeer and fired. Instantly the herd took flight. He fired again, twice, apparently missing all three times. Disgusted and disheartened, Poulsson trudged across to where the target animal had been standing. The snow there was stained red. Quickening his pace, he followed the tracks up to the crest of a nearby ridge, and just over the top he found the wounded reindeer thrashing about on its side. One more shot and the animal was dead.

Poulsson pulled a cup out of his rucksack and drank as much of the reindeer's blood as he could before it froze, then set about dismembering the animal. The sun was al-most down by the time he had packed his rucksack with about 70 pounds of meat, organs and bones.

Back at the cabin, his three companions looked up listlessly as he entered. They expected nothing. Then one of them noticed the blood on his white ski outfit, and with whoops of joy they fell upon the rucksack. "We had a very, very good Christmas after all," Poulsson said. "When we had finished with that reindeer there was nothing left but the hide and a pile of bones. None of us felt any revulsion about eating everything of the animal that could be eaten; when you are as hungry as we were, you are not fussy."

While Poulsson's advance party was barely managing to survive, six more Norwegian saboteurs were being trained in Scotland for the attack on the hydroelectric plant. These agents finally parachuted onto the Hardanger Plateau on the night of February 17, 1943. They were almost immediately trapped by the worst blizzard any of them had ever experienced; five days passed before the gale-force winds abated. But the two groups finally managed to join up. "It was a great moment," Poulsson recalled. "They gave us things like chocolate and raisins and other civilized food and we offered to serve them reindeer, but they didn't appreciate it much."

With an attack now possible, the saboteurs wasted no

Steel scaffolding is all that remains of the glass-roofed Forum arena in Copenhagen after it was sabotaged in 1943 by resistants who hid a bomb in a beer crate. The building was chosen as a target because it was being converted into a barracks for German Occupation troops.

A German Army truck, turned into a flaming juggernaut by saboteurs, leaves a trail of burning fuel along an Amsterdam street. Although the technique of destruction used in this case is not known, vehicles were usually sabotaged by grenades or homemade bombs.

time. Leaving Knut Haugland behind to maintain radio contact with London, Poulsson and the rest of the men skied with rucksacks full of equipment to the original cabin at the edge of the plateau, within two miles of the power station on the opposite side of a deep gorge.

The fortress-like, seven-story Norsk hydro plant stood on a rock platform blasted out of an almost sheer mountain wall. It could be approached from only three directions: by way of a narrow suspension bridge spanning the gorge; along a single-track railway hewn into the side of the ravine and running directly into the plant; or from above, down steep steps alongside the 12 huge holding basins that fed water into the turbines of the plant from a lake at the top of the mountains.

Both the bridge and the basins were patrolled by sentries continually, but the railway approach was not guarded, as the gorge was thought too steep to climb. The men chose to climb up to the railway track under cover of darkness.

None of the young Norwegians had any illusions about the risks. "I don't think any of us really expected to get out of there alive," Poulsson said. "Personally, I thought we would probably be able to do the job, but I didn't imagine we would be able to escape."

The attack was planned for a Saturday night, February 27.

It would be made by two two-man demolition parties, with the remaining five providing cover. At 8 o'clock they were ready to go. Claus Helberg, one of the Rjukan natives who knew the area perfectly, led the way: first a long, straight schuss down the mountain, then a trek through a thick wood and onto a road snaking into the valley. No one spoke; there was nothing to say.

The men heard the deep hum of the hydro plant before they caught sight of it, looming huge in the moonlight far below them on the other side of the gorge. Soon they left the road again, clambering and slithering down a steep slope to a small clearing in a wood; there they hid their rucksacks, skis and poles under the snow in the hope of retrieving them on the way back. From then on, they carried only the explosive and fuses, their Tommy guns and pistols, and a pair of heavy metal-cutting shears to hack through the steel fence surrounding the plant.

They descended deeper into the valley over slippery rock made even more treacherous in the dark. At the bottom of the gorge they crossed the river by means of a bridge of ice and then faced the final obstacle between them and their target, a 600-foot climb up a steep rock face with only outcrops of spruce and pine to hint that it could be climbed at all. It was every man for himself up that rock face, each of

155

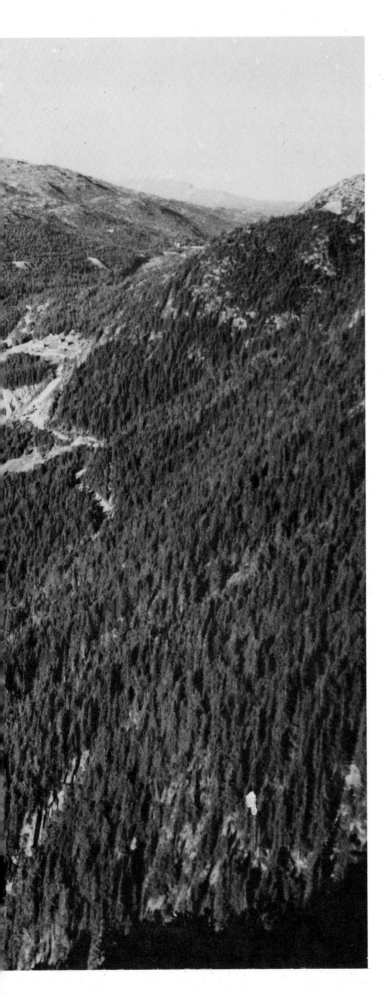

them finding his own route, hand by hand, foot by foot. The noise they made was muffled by the hum of the plant's turbines and a rising wind. Shortly after 11 o'clock, the last man heaved himself over the brink of the ledge onto the railway track. They rested for a few moments, hearts pounding, before setting off once again along the track toward the hydro plant.

Silently and in single file, they moved up to the shelter of a small transformer station only a few hundred yards from the plant. At 12:30, Arne Kjelstrup, the Oslo plumber, crept up to the perimeter fence with his heavy shears, expertly snipped the chain around a gate and cautiously pushed it open. The others followed him through. Then the two-man demolition parties separated to look for access into the basement, where they knew they would find the vital electrolysis tanks that separated the elements making up ordinary water and left a high concentration of heavy water. The first pair crawled into the basement through a cable tunnel just wide enough to admit them. A startled Norwegian night watchman on duty in the basement was only too happy to get out of their way. But as they went to work fixing the charges, the sound of shattering glass sent them diving for cover. It was the second demolition team breaking in.

The saboteurs wrapped their plastic charges around the 18 electrolysis tanks, which were about four feet high, 12 inches in diameter and protected by stainless-steel jackets. "Our explosives fit around the apparatus like a glove," recalled demolition chief Joachim Rönneberg. "You just pressed them around and against the cylindrical metal containers, and they stuck." He then inserted pencil-like fuses in the 18 plastic globs and pinched their ends, activating the fuses. The whole works was timed to go off in 30 seconds. The demolition teams hurried the watchman to safety up a flight of stairs, then dashed through a steel door that they had already opened from the inside as an escape route.

Wrapping the tanks with the explosive and setting the fuses had taken about 25 minutes, but to the men in the covering party waiting outside it had seemed like hours. Poulsson was hiding with a saboteur named Knut Haukelid close to the barracks used by the German guards. "We couldn't understand what had happened," Poulsson recalled, "and then we heard this very small, muffled bang. I thought it had not worked, it could not be the real thing. At

The Norsk Hydro electric plant, target of the most important sabotage operation in Norway, is set beside the deep gorge of the Mana River, 70 miles west of Oslo. The plant, Germany's main source of so-called heavy water needed for atomic research, was so closely guarded that saboteurs had to approach it by a seemingly impossible route: down the slope at right, across a natural bridge of ice at the bottom of the ravine (lower left) and up a cliffside so steep that local villagers never climbed it.

157

that moment, a German soldier came out of the hut with a torch and started to shine it around where we were hiding. I was very tempted to shoot him, but I looked at Haukelid and he shook his head. It was a very good thing I didn't kill him because the alarm had still not been raised. After looking around a bit with his torch, he went back into the hut and shut the door."

The saboteurs had been twice lucky: the explosion had not only been muffled by the plant's thick concrete wall; it also sounded like a noise that was routinely made by some special equipment on the plant's upper balconies. The men did not care to question their luck. They raced down the railway track and were halfway across the river at the bottom of the gorge before the sirens began to wail. And they were well away—high and safe on the mountain across the gorge—when they saw the headlights of the trucks bringing up German reinforcements from Rjukan. (Eventually all the saboteurs made good their escape, most of them by skiing cross-country some 250 miles to neutral Sweden.)

The Germans were furious. General Nikolaus von Falkenhorst, Supreme Commander in Norway, rushed to the scene to inspect the damage for himself and was so infuriated by what he found that he berated the German guards in front of a delighted group of Norwegian onlookers. Afterward Falkenhorst grudgingly conceded to an associate that the raid was "the finest coup I have seen in this War."

London received the news in a brief message from Knut Haugland: "Operation carried out with complete success. High concentration plant completely destroyed. No suspicions aroused and no shots exchanged. Greetings."

The daring raid had several anticlimaxes. Although the damage it caused was extensive and 1,000 pounds of precious heavy water, representing more than three months' production, had been lost, the Germans were able—by working day and night—to get the output of heavy water started again by early summer. In mid-1943 U.S. atomic scientists were increasingly convinced that an atomic bomb of astonishing destructiveness could be built, and it seemed vital to forestall the German manufacture of such a weapon. A second attempt to sabotage the hydro plant appeared to be out of the question, since the Germans had redoubled their security measures there. After much debate, the Allied high command ordered an air raid. The 153-plane bombing mission did just enough damage to persuade the Germans to close up the Rjukan heavy-water operation.

Soon a message came in from Norway informing Allied intelligence that the Germans were planning to move their entire supply of heavy water to Germany by rail and sea. Perhaps it could be destroyed while in transit. Knut Haukelid, the last member of the original sabotage team still in the area, was alerted. He and two recruits from the local Resistance began to map their strategy.

It appeared to be impossible to blow up the railway freight cars that would take the drums of heavy water from the hydroelectric plant to the dock at Mael; a large detachment of German soldiers would guard the train and the right-of-way. However, something might be done to the large ferry that would carry the flatcars across Tinn Lake before they proceeded again by rail to the port of Heroya. To their surprise, Haukelid and his men discovered that the ferry slip was lightly guarded. The night before the shipment was due to depart, they boarded the ferry *Hydro* as passengers, placed a 12-foot-long, sausage-shaped charge of plastic explosive inside her hull, and set a time fuse that gave them a long head start toward Sweden.

Shortly after 10 o'clock the next morning, the *Hydro* chugged out into the lake; the flatcars, carrying 39 drums of heavy water, were lashed to her deck. There were 53 people on board, including civilian passengers, crew and German soldiers. At 10:45, a huge explosion ripped open the bow of the ferry. As the ship keeled over, the flatcars broke loose, rolled off the deck and plunged into 1,300 feet of water—far too deep for salvage. A few minutes later the *Hydro* sank. Twenty-six people went down with her. But the loss of the heavy water so dispirited German scientists that their atomic research never recovered its impetus.

The Norsk raid was unique in its sustained efforts, its hardships, and the importance it was accorded by Allied intelligence chiefs. But saboteurs in all of the occupied countries were routinely setting off bangs that—taken together—amounted to a major contribution to the overall war effort.

In Denmark, where Resistance groups had little heavy industry to destroy, one of the biggest coups was pulled off by three employees of the Luftwaffe's great air base at Aalborg. In preparation for the job, the conspirators smuggled large quantities of explosive past the guards in their lunch pails. By leaving out the usual sandwiches and going hungry for three weeks, they brought in enough plastic explosive to blow the place sky-high. One day in the autumn of 1944, they spent their lunch hour attaching charges with delayed-action fuses to everything within reach. The explosions started that night and continued for 12 hours, destroying 40 Luftwaffe planes, fuel stores, workshops, offices and canteens.

Belgian saboteurs proved to be particularly adept at obtaining explosives, arms and other supplies from the most convenient source: German installations. Resistance networks stole tons of dynamite from German-operated quarries and mines, and one especially daring group looted the national arms factory at Herstal, walking off with a big haul of dynamite, detonators and rifles. And the Belgians used their purloined explosives with telling effect. One network, known as Group G, specialized in sabotaging high-voltage lines; the damage caused by repeated attacks was so extensive that repair work cost the Germans more than 20 million man-hours of labor.

But it was in France that saboteurs reaped their richest harvest. France was not only the biggest and most heavily industrialized of the occupied nations; it was also the most important in its strategic location, dominating Western Europe. The well-developed French railroad system was under constant attack by saboteurs intent on disrupting the movement of German troops and matériel through France and to the Low Countries and Italy. But one Resistance network, operating near the Swiss border, specialized in a different kind of transportation sabotage, with momentous—albeit little-publicized—results.

This outfit, code-named Armada, sabotaged vital links in the extensive French canal system in the summer of 1943, just when the Germans needed it to move small naval vessels—torpedo boats and miniature submarines—from their North Sea ports to Italy in anticipation of the Allied invasion there. The damage done to the canals substantially reduced the cost of the Italian campaign to the Allies, and it also interrupted the transport of goods needed by the German war machine.

The saboteurs, led by Raymond Basset, began operations against the canals in July of 1943. On the night of July 26, three men blew a big hole in a dam and lock on a canal at Chalon-sur-Saône, draining a long section of the waterway and stranding many barges. Two weeks later, the Briare Canal, which was being used to circumnavigate the blockage at Chalon, was put out of action when two locks were destroyed by a single saboteur. This time 3,000 barges were stranded. Two days later, locks west of Toul, on the Marne-Rhine Canal, were blown up by the same man, and two long sections of the canal were drained of water. And after the Germans had spent four months repairing the damage to the dam and lock at Chalon, the saboteurs cheekily returned and blew it up again.

In the fertile field of industrial sabotage, a young SOE agent named Harry Rée pioneered an ingenious variation

An American officer, one of 100 men airdropped into France by the OSS prior to the Allied invasion, instructs maquisards of the Drôme department in the use of an automatic pistol. The arrival of the OSS agents made a great impression on farmers and villagers in remote areas. Said one old Frenchman in amazement, "To think that General Eisenhower thought enough of our little village to send an American officer here to help us."

THE SCHOOLBOY SABOTEURS

"If the grownups won't do something, we will" was the battle cry of 11 intrepid teenagers from Denmark's Aalborg Cathedral School. In 1941 they founded the Churchill Club, a resistance unit named after the doughty British leader. The club churned out subversive newsletters on a toy printing press, filched weapons that German soldiers carelessly left near barracks windows or in public cloakrooms, and conducted dozens of sabotage missions.

Their targets usually were chosen on the spur of the moment. One time, several of the boys were hitching a ride uphill on the tailboard of a German truck when they found a hoard of war matériel under a load of hay. They lost no time setting fire to the hay and disembarking. On another occasion, a 14-year-old member accomplished a true masterpiece of arson when a blaze he started with a single well-placed match destroyed an entire train bearing German military supplies.

In May of 1942, a weapon-stealing foray landed the boys in jail, but they refused to quit. With a file smuggled in by a visitor, they sawed through their cell bars. But instead of escaping, they used the jail as their headquarters; night after night, they stuffed clothing under their blankets to resemble sleeping bodies, slipped out for sabotage, then returned before dawn. After two months, the boys were caught returning and sent to a no-nonsense prison. But by that time their derring-do had become so well known that an underground comic strip called *The Boy Saboteurs* was being circulated throughout Denmark, inspiring other Danish youths to organize Churchill Clubs of their own.

on the normal hit-and-run attacks. Rée, the leader of a network code-named Stockbroker, first set his sights on the largest war plant in his area of eastern France: the Peugeot automobile factory at Sochaux, near the Swiss border. The plant had been converted by the Germans to the manufacture of tank turrets and aircraft engine components. On the night of July 14, 1943, the RAF had tried to smash the Sochaux factory, but most of the bombs missed the target and more than 100 townspeople were killed. Production was unaffected.

After the raid, Rée arranged a secret meeting with the head of the house of Peugeot, Rudolphe, and quietly suggested that he should help sabotage his own industrial complex. Otherwise, argued Rée, the RAF would return, possibly doing the factory more damage than the sabotage would, and certainly killing more townspeople.

Peugeot was incredulous at first, then suspicious, fearing Rée might be a German agent testing his loyalty to the Reich. To reassure Peugeot that he was acting on behalf of the Allies, Rée offered to have the BBC repeat any phrase Peugeot chose on one of its nightly French-language broadcasts. Peugeot decided upon the sentence, "Benedictine is a sweet liqueur." Two nights later, the phrase was broadcast, along with dozens of other enigmatic messages that were coded signals to French Resistance groups.

Peugeot, now convinced that Rée was a bona fide Allied agent, agreed to help put his own factory out of commission. He gave Rée floor plans of the plant and put him in touch with some trustworthy employees. Plastic explosive was smuggled into the Peugeot works, and on the night of November 5, 1943, the cooperating factory hands wrapped the stuff around the most valuable and vulnerable machinery—steel presses, electrical transformers and the like.

At 10 minutes past midnight, the Peugeot works was blasted by a series of heavy explosions. The factory was out of production for many weeks. The Germans twice shipped in replacements for the steel presses used to fabricate tank turrets, and Rée and his network twice blew them up before they could be unloaded from the trucks and canal barges that had transported them from Germany.

Not long after these triumphs, Rée ran into a Gestapo trap at the house of a contact. He proved to be as gritty as he was guileful. A German with a revolver greeted him when he knocked on the door. Rée entered innocently, imperturbably invited the German to have a drink, then hit him over the head with the bottle as hard as he could. But the German did not go down. Instead, he jumped from his chair and, as Rée recalled, "pushed his pistol against my ribs. I could feel it digging into me. I heard shots, but I did not feel any impact."

After a long, fierce struggle, Rée managed to bash the German's head against a stone wall. Then he stumbled out of the house and made his way some four miles to the home of another Resistance contact. There, a doctor discovered that Rée had three bullet wounds in his body. Two of the bullets had pierced his lungs and one had grazed his heart. Rée's life was saved by members of the French Resistance who helped him cross the border to reach a hospital in Switzerland. Finally, in the summer of 1944, Rée was able to return to England.

Another network used Rée's form of persuasion successfully on the Dunlop tire factory at Montluçon in central France in March 1944. Dunlop's managing director and a

A Danish boy runs for cover as a munitions works in Copenhagen is wracked by explosions set off by a team of 30 saboteurs in mid-1944. The resistants, members of a large network known as the "Middle-Class Partisans," rode past the main gate of the plant inside trucks identified as ambulances and fire-fighting vehicles. The assault force then subdued the guards and gathered all the workers together in an open space on the plant grounds, instructing them to run for it when they heard the sound of the factory sirens. Within a few minutes, the sirens blared, the workers fled for their lives and five great explosions left the plant in flaming ruins, with only the walls still standing. Not a single shot had been fired.

sizable number of workers collaborated in the plant's destruction, bringing the explosives into the factory yard in the company's own trucks.

The technique was tried yet again on Dunlop's competitors, the Michelin tire firm, but the Michelin family declined to cooperate in the sabotage of their factory at Clermont-Ferrand. The agent who had made the approach then radioed a request that the RAF raid the plant. If no bombing raid was forthcoming, he pointed out, the self-sabotage tactic would never work again. The RAF promptly obliged, sending waves of bombers that wrecked large sections of the sprawling plant.

One of the most successful saboteurs in France, and undoubtedly the most flamboyant, was an operator known to his admiring men as "Capitaine Michel." His name was Michael Trotobas, and he had been brought up by his French parents in the English seaside resort of Brighton. Trotobas had developed a taste for the seamy underside of Brighton life; a lean, good-looking man with a raffish pencil mustache, he might have been taken for a gambler or pool shark himself. And when he parachuted into France in early 1943 and settled in the grim industrial city of Lille, some 120 miles northeast of Paris, he naturally drew some rather shady patriots to his cause. Another SOE agent on a visit to Lille sought out Trotobas and was directed to a factory worker's home, where he found the agent simultaneously enjoying a hot bath and conducting a loud argument with a gaggle of notorious racetrack touts.

Trotobas knew what he was doing. The gravest danger to SOE agents was loose talk that might be overheard by informers or German counteragents. Trotobas deliberately chose to work with men who understood the importance of keeping their mouths shut, and he soon assembled a large and efficient network of reliable saboteurs. His touts and gamblers were also acquainted with patriotic members of the local French police, who told them which gendarmes were pro-German and warned them when the German police were doing anything unusual. On at least one occasion, the friendly gendarmes loaned the saboteurs perfect disguises—policemen's uniforms.

Trotobas's network, code-named Farmer, scored its first major success in late February of 1943, when 40 railroad freight cars jumped the sabotaged tracks on the busy Lens-Bethune line, halting all traffic for two days. By midsummer, Farmer's railroad specialists were causing 15 or 20 derailments a week. Both sides of the Amiens-Arras line, according to one observer, were "absolutely littered with damaged trucks, carriages and material."

Trotobas and his partners also struck nearby industrial plants that supplied the Germans: machine-tool factories in the town of Armentières, textile mills in Roubaix and the largest tannery in Cambrai. And to vary the fare, Trotobas led the saboteurs on what he humorously called "tourist jaunts" to the closely guarded ports of Calais and Boulogne on the English Channel, and to Amiens on the Somme River. There, his bangs destroyed sundry naval installations.

Trotobas's most impressive bit of sabotage was carried out against the locomotive works at Fives, an eastern suburb of Lille, one of the largest facilities of its kind in France. The German railway system, which was being bludgeoned by Allied air attacks in the summer of 1943, was relying more and more upon French and Belgian railroad repair and production centers. Aware of this, RAF intelligence was in favor of sending a fleet of bombers to reduce Fives. But SOE argued against an air attack, on the ground that the locomotive works was flanked by densely settled residential districts. So the agency was given an opportunity to destroy the facility first.

Trotobas took 20 men with him to Fives on the night of June 27. They walked casually up to the gate of the enormous locomotive works wearing French police uniforms borrowed from their gendarme friends. Trotobas, dressed in a natty suit, flashed a forged Gestapo pass and announced that the group had come to inspect the shop's security arrangements. The watchmen admitted the whole entourage—and the saboteurs quickly proceeded to load the shop's electrical system and other sensitive equipment with plastic explosive.

Trotobas and his men were walking out of the main gate when one of their plastic charges exploded prematurely. Unruffled, Trotobas ordered the watchmen not to call for help until he returned with teams of firemen and German officials. He and his bogus gendarmes then melted into the night while the locomotive works continued to explode, rocking the eastern sections of Lille. Fires raged until the next afternoon.

According to one story, certain RAF intelligence officers doubted that the Fives plant had been destroyed. So SOE headquarters radioed Trotobas: "Please send photographs." Trotobas obtained a camera and a forged document that identified him as an insurance-company inspector. Displaying his fake credentials, he talked his way past a cordon of SD agents: his firm, he said, needed pictures to help assess the damage. He took his snapshots and calmly walked away from the smoldering locomotive works. Once developed, the photographs were forwarded to RAF headquarters in London by secret courier. Attached to them was a card that read, "With the compliments of the Resistance."

By the autumn of 1943, the German authorities in northeastern France were desperate to break up the Farmer organization and nab its leader. Trotobas's shady operatives maintained tight security. But Farmer had a weak spot, an agent code-named "Olivier" who had been sent out by SOE to join Trotobas's spirited network of saboteurs. Trotobas did not trust Olivier; he was, Trotobas said, "too much of a matador," taking needless risks to show off his courage.

Trotobas was right. When a subagent from another network shot a German soldier, Olivier helped him to escape the Arras neighborhood. But something went wrong. The German police caught the subagent and extracted from him—after torture—the address of a house in Arras where he had hidden before fleeing the area. The Germans raided the house and captured Olivier, who was spending the night there. Olivier, despite his customary bravado, submitted meekly to arrest and, after being beaten by his captors, gave the Germans the address of another house where Trotobas had stayed.

Olivier may have considered the information harmless; he had reason to think that Trotobas was no longer there. Unfortunately, Trotobas was indeed on the premises when the police raided the house, and he greeted them with a fusillade of shots, killing the inspector who headed the raid. But Trotobas, too, died in the shoot-out, along with a girl who was trapped in the house with him.

Trotobas had organized Farmer so well that it continued to function without him: In one subsequent operation, the network destroyed 11 railroad locomotives. Nor was Trotobas forgotten. The townspeople of Lille honored his contribution to the Allies' war effort—and indirectly paid homage to saboteurs all over the world—by naming a street Rue Capitaine Michel.

FRANCE'S GUERRILLA LEGIONS

Armed with a German-made rifle of World War I vintage, a Resistance sharpshooter lurks in ambush among the branches of a tree somewhere in Normandy.

FROM DRAFT DODGERS TO RESISTANCE HEROES

"Men who come to fight live badly, in precarious fashion, with food hard to find," warned a recruiting leaflet put out by one of the French guerrilla bands known as maquis. "They will be absolutely cut off from their families for the duration; the enemy does not apply the rules of war to them; they cannot be assured any pay; all correspondence is forbidden." In less desperate times, this description might have served to repel potential recruits rather than attract them. But the Vichy government had already presented able-bodied Frenchmen an even bleaker future early in 1943: all males more than 20 years old were to report for labor in German factories and defense installations—under conditions known to be prison-like.

Instead of registering for Vichy's labor draft, thousands of men headed for the mountains and wild places of France—chiefly in Brittany and the south—and joined the scores of fighting units or small groups of fugitives who had preceded them. Because some groups gave the maquis a bad name by raiding local farms and villages for food, clothing and tobacco, the young draft dodgers not only had to wage the patriotic war against the Germans and Vichy collaborators, but in many cases also had to fight an uphill battle to win the support of their countrymen. Dozens of maquisards with cameras recorded their units' Resistance activities in pictures like the ones that appear on these pages, and some of their photographs were secretly circulated throughout France or smuggled out to the Allies.

As they improved in numbers and training, maquisard teams of saboteurs and raiders began ranging far and wide from their wilderness strongholds, and more and more local people supplied them with food and information on German troop movements. The maquis war would not reach its peak until the Allies invaded France in June 1944. But, as one leader said, his men were "ready for anything that would satisfy their thirst for action and revenge." To some of the maquisards, nothing mattered but a chance at the Germans. Said one, "I have three children, and a good wife of whom I am fond. But I like the war better."

Waiting to receive messages broadcast to them by the BBC in code, uniformed maquisards enjoy the comfort of a farmhouse in the Loire Valley.

A typically ill-equipped maquisard guards a Brittany road. His straw boots were discarded by a German who had worn them for warmth on the Eastern Front.

Four volunteers, leaving home to enlist in a maquis, were photographed from the rear in order to prevent identification and reprisals against their relatives.

At a maquis retreat deep inside a forest, new recruits are sworn in. They have stripped a sapling for a flagpole to hoist a banner bearing a cross of Lorraine.

Maquisards in the mountains raise a roof over a more-or-less permanent barracks. For the sake of safety, some maquis moved their camp every few weeks.

THE BUILDING OF A MAQUIS

The growth of any maquis from a small gang to a large and effective fighting force came slowly and depended mainly on two factors: the availability of weapons and the quality of the leader.

Groups generally began with few arms, and poorly led bands languished in demoralized squalor. But strong leaders soon disciplined raw recruits, trained them in tactics, had them build camps and sent them on night raids to capture rifles from French police stations and German outposts.

Units that managed to follow a maquis motto—"Each weapon should bring in at least one other weapon each week"—attracted the lion's share of new volunteers and expanded rapidly.

A REGIMEN OF HAZARDOUS DUTIES

Daily life in a maquis involved many assignments that were only slightly less hazardous than sabotage missions. Couriers delivered encoded messages exchanging information and coordinating operations with other Resistance units, and groups of maquisards canvassed the area in search of food and supplies. Each man risked betrayal by collaborators, capture by the Germans and torture that could force him to reveal his comrades' whereabouts.

To prevent unnecessary risk, many a maquis imposed strict security measures and dealt harshly with disobedient members. A member of a 200-man maquis in northern France reported just how seriously a breach of discipline was taken: "When we discovered that a boy had gone down to the village for a drink in the local café, not once, but twice, I said that he should be judged. We had a council of war with a free vote. I voted for the death penalty. That was the way it went.

"Right up to the end, when we were tying him to a tree, the boy could not believe we were going to shoot him. I think we were right to do what we did."

Foraging maquisards of the department of Drôme wolf down lunch at the home of a friendly farmer.

In the hope of making threadbare clothing last a while longer, a maquisard in the Haute-Loire applies an emergency patch to the seat of a comrade's trousers.

Maquisards buy food from a woman with ration tickets given them by a townsman. Since they were outlaws, they were never issued ration cards of their own.

STRIKING AT TARGETS OF OPPORTUNITY

After a few months of on-the-job training, the men of a maquis became past masters at the techniques of guerrilla warfare. They employed silence and surprise to best advantage, coming and going by different routes, quietly dispatching German sentries with a knife or a wire garrote whenever possible. Leaving nothing to chance, they developed a network of clandestine patriots—local gendarmes, postmistresses and railway workers who regularly provided them with advance notice of enemy patrols and of the movement of German troops and matériel in the vicinity.

This information proved to be especially important for railroad sabotage; a badly timed derailment might take the lives of innocent French passengers rather than interrupting German operations.

Though maquisards sometimes derailed

A local postmistress telephones reports of German troop movements to maquisards in the Haute-Loire.

A wounded leader maps out a raid for his members—among them one of the few women maquisards.

Mounting an ambush, maquisards advance on

trains by the laborious process of raising tracks, they increasingly relied on explosives air-dropped by the Allies. Plastic explosive was marvelously efficient; a small quantity of the doughlike stuff usually destroyed enough track to derail a train traveling at normal speed. In fact the explosive was so effective that it sometimes proved dangerous to the maquisards. On one mission, several saboteurs waiting to admire their work at a point 200 yards away were startled when the blast sent a huge chunk of railroad track whizzing past them.

One bold maquisard used a novel method to halt railroad traffic at the Miserey-Salines station near Besançon. After derailing one train by tearing up a length of track, he commandeered four trains and forced the railway men to send them hurtling into the wreckage. This pileup, which interrupted rail transportation for weeks, was so extensive that sightseers flocked from all over, and it came to be known as "the mountain of Miserey."

A maquisard uses a truck for cover from German fire during operations in Dreux, 45 miles from Paris.

ouse reportedly frequented by German soldiers.

Sabotaging a rail line, one maquisard plants plastic explosive on the track while comrades stand guard.

Members of the powerful Vercors maquis assemble at a bridge they blasted to hamper the Germans. Some of the maquisards are equipped with air-droppe

A locomotive teeters on the edge of a bridge blown by a maquis to block essential German transport in the Limousin mountains.

J.S. Army combat gear.

An Italian-built Luftwaffe fighter sabotaged by maquisards lies wrecked on a field near the city of Limoges in the Haute-Vienne.

The coffin of a maquisard killed in the Pyrenees is brought down by mule.

DIE-HARD FIGHTERS FOR THE CAUSE

A bullet to the brain was often the fate of maquisards who were captured by the Germans. As a result, they fought to the death, and some even were prepared to cut their own wrists to avoid capture and torture that could wring from them information fatal to their fellows.

Yet in dying a martyr's death, a maquisard might strengthen the resolve of others to go on fighting. So it was with a 20-year-old recruit known only as Nono. With the leader of his maquis in east-central France, Nono set out in the summer of 1944 to sabotage a heavily guarded German fuel train near the Ognon River. Before the two maquisards could reach their target, a German patrol spotted them and shot Nono in the leg. Nevertheless, he managed to get up and draw some of the Germans off on a chase while the leader made his way to safety. When the Germans caught up with Nono, he engaged them in a lopsided shooting match. Within minutes, Nono lay riddled with bullets.

The body of the young maquisard was carried to the village of Bonnay. There it attracted the largest crowd of mourners ever seen at a funeral in the region: 3,000 citizens and a full-dress maquis guard of honor toting Sten guns. "His dead body," said Nono's proud leader, "was an inspiration to the valley."

Maquisards pay their last respects before the secluded woodland graves of

comrades who died fighting for the Vercors maquis. In front of the conventional cross that marks the grave at right stands a patriotic cross of Lorraine.

On November 11, 1943, the 280 resistants of a maquis in east-central France thumbed their noses at the Germans with a daring celebration of Armistice Day, the erstwhile national holiday that marked the Allies' victory over Germany in the First World War. Far from being a reckless stunt, the celebration was a carefully planned and precisely executed military operation. The leader of the guerrilla group, a former French Army colonel named Jean Romans-Petit, left nothing to chance. As an arena for the forbidden festivities, he chose the small town of Oyonnax, but a week before Armistice Day he decoyed the authorities by plastering the village of Nantua, 12 miles away, with illegal posters calling for a demonstration there on November 11.

Just as Romans-Petit had expected, the police station at Oyonnax was stripped of its gendarmes to provide Nantua with reinforcements, and in the early hours of Armistice Day, the maquisards—bringing along cameras to record the event for posterity *(page 180-181)*—went into action. They swept down from their hillside lairs, seized Oyonnax and posted guards to block traffic in or out of town. Next, the maquisards proceeded to capture the police station, the town hall and the telephone exchange, all without incident. Then they marched to the town's memorial to the soldiers who had died in the last war. There, in the midst of a cheering and weeping crowd, Romans-Petit placed at the foot of the statue a floral cross of Lorraine inscribed to "the victors of yesterday from those of tomorrow." After leading the citizens in a rousing rendition of the "Marseillaise," the maquisards left the village and melted away into the hills.

The brief but glorious liberation of the little town was the opening shot in a nationwide maquis offensive that would escalate wildly in the following months and culminate in full-scale insurrection and widespread sabotage throughout France. News of the guerrilla group's exploit spread rapidly and filled Frenchmen everywhere with pride and glee. Even more important, it bolstered the spirits of the maquisards themselves, which were then at low ebb.

By that cold and dismal November, many thousands of young Frenchmen had fled into the hills to join one of the numerous maquis and to evade the sweeping labor draft required by the Germans the previous February. Some of the guerrilla bands were as well-organized and aggressive as Colonel Romans-Petit's group; these units were generally

7

UP FROM THE UNDERGROUND

led by former French Army officers or air-dropped SOE men. But many maquis were made up of underfed and poorly clothed youths, much given to bickering and to petty jealousies. "Most of the time we were cold, wet and hungry," recalled the leader of a small maquis in the Haute-Saône. "We did not dare build a fire in case the smoke gave away our location, so we rarely had hot food to eat, and if it rained we had no means of drying our clothes. We never bothered to make waterproof shelters in the forest because we moved camp about every two weeks to avoid being discovered. For days on end we lived in wet clothes, and slept in them too. An hour's good weather was like a gift, a real bonus. The maquisard who was properly fed and had decent dry clothing was a rare creature indeed."

The worst part of the maquisards' plight was their lack of serviceable weapons. In the department of Montagne Noire in southern France, a maquis of more than 300 men shared two submachine guns and 60 rifles. In the department of Lot in southwest France, a maquis of 30 men possessed one Sten gun with 100 rounds of ammunition, three rifles with five rounds each and 10 revolvers with 10 rounds each. Another group of 30 men near Cahors had only one rifle and 10 rounds among them.

Most of the maquisards were bitterly disappointed by the few and meager airdrops of arms from the Allies. Some 600 drop zones had been prepared throughout France to receive *parachutages,* and every night during the period of full moon, reception committees stood by, hoping and praying for the distant drone of a drop plane. But time after time, when the first pale tinge of dawn appeared on the horizon, the maquisards stole back to their mountain lairs empty-handed. During the last three months of 1943, only 107 RAF sorties were flown to France, and a large portion of the puny 139 tons of supplies they dropped was intercepted by Occupation forces.

There were several reasons for the Allies' poor showing so far. November and December of 1943 were especially stormy months, and air operations were severely affected. Besides, the strategic bombing of Germany had been assigned top priority, and the Allies were unwilling to divert precious aircraft for dropping arms to untrained guerrillas. Although the United States donated a large part of the supplies, it provided only three transport planes. As a result,

23 Halifaxes of the RAF had to bear almost the entire burden of supplying all underground forces throughout the whole of northwestern Europe.

Nevertheless, substantial aid was on its way to the maquis by the end of 1943. Three men, all of them veterans of the French Resistance, helped to make it possible in separate appeals to Prime Minister Winston Churchill.

Emmanuel d'Astier, the former head of the resistance network called Libération, first broached the subject of aid to the maquis in early December, 1943. At the time, Churchill was convalescing in Marrakesh after being taken ill on his way back from Teheran, where he had met with President Franklin D. Roosevelt and Soviet leader Josef Stalin to discuss plans for the invasion of Europe. D'Astier, who made frequent trips to North Africa to coordinate with the Free French forces in training there, asked to have an interview with Churchill. He was an eloquent speaker, and his description of the plight of the maquisards made a deep impression on the Prime Minister.

When Churchill arrived back in London some six weeks later, a quiet, gray-haired French lawyer named Michel Brault asked to speak with him. Brault was responsible for running a clandestine relief organization called Service Maquis, which was attempting to supply the big maquis groups throughout France with food, clothing and medicine. He had visited dozens of maquis camps to take the measure of the guerrillas' problems, and his soft-spoken but passionate appeal to Churchill prompted the British leader to call a conference of ministers at 10 Downing Street. The ministers met on January 27, 1944, and agreed that airdrops to the maquis were to rank second only to the bombing of Germany on the RAF's priority list.

That agreement was translated into action four days later by Tommy Yeo-Thomas—the SOE agent who had worked with Jean Moulin to unify French resistance. Ever since his return from France in November, Yeo-Thomas had been pleading the cause of the maquis, but with so little success that he was on the point of resigning from SOE in disgust. In a last attempt to help his friends in France, he had asked to see Churchill. When Yeo-Thomas was ushered into the Cabinet Room at Downing Street, he found the Prime Minister seated alone at a long table, smoking a cigar. "I'm a busy man and I have no time to waste," Churchill growled. "I'm told you know France better than any other Englishman. I doubt it. What have you got to say? I can give you five minutes."

The five minutes turned into an hour. Yeo-Thomas commenced a detailed description of the living conditions in the maquis. Before he finished, the Prime Minister interrupted him in order to dictate a memo to the Air Ministry directing that 100 aircraft be put at the disposal of SOE's French section.

Churchill's new policy toward the maquis was only partly a response to the eloquence of d'Astier, Brault and Yeo-Thomas. Allied preparations for the invasion of occupied Europe were maturing rapidly, and Churchill had already realized that widespread maquis sabotage would be enormously helpful to the assault troops landing in Normandy. In furtherance of this role, the RAF and two Liberator squadrons of the U.S. Army Air Forces flew 759 missions to supply the maquis during the first three months of 1944—a sevenfold increase over the previous quarter. The maquisards, interpreting the airborne bonanzas as a sign that the long-awaited invasion was not very far off, stepped up their campaign of sabotage.

There was another reason, equally compelling, for the upsurge in activity by the maquis. The maquisards were becoming increasingly outraged by their enemy, the Milice, the paramilitary force of Fascist Frenchmen that served the Germans as a tool of terror. The ranks of the Milice were filled with thugs and cutthroats whose viciousness often surpassed even that of the German Gestapo and SS. Early in 1944, *Défense de la France*, a leading newspaper of the underground, called on its readership to take drastic action against the Milice: "Kill the Miliciens, exterminate them, because they have deliberately chosen the road of treason. Strike them down like mad dogs. Destroy them as you would vermin. Kill without passion and without hate. Kill without pity or remorse, because it is our duty."

By then, the Milice comprised some 45,000 toughs and Fascist fanatics. They were spoiling for a showdown with the maquis—and they soon got it. For nearly a month, a force of about 4,500 Miliciens and members of a similar Vichy force called the Garde Mobile had been attempting to clear the maquis from the departments of Ain and Haute-Savoie in southeastern France. To escape the dragnet, hundreds of maquisards had withdrawn onto the snow-covered Glières Plateau, a natural Alpine citadel that was protected by steep, sheer rock and accessible only on foot along rough mountain tracks. Lieutenant Théodose Morel, the commander of the beleaguered maquisards, viewed the plateau as more than a refuge. He regarded it as a national redoubt—a patch of France where patriots would be able to gather strength until they were ready to liberate the whole country. It was a wild and perhaps foolish dream, but men died gallantly in its cause.

Early in February, Morel ceremoniously inaugurated his campaign of liberation. To the assembled guerrillas of the self-styled Glières battalion, he declared: "My comrades, men of the united Battalion of Glières. This is the first corner of France to be free. The future will not be easy for any of us, but whatever the outcome of what we are doing now, I know that you will face it in a way befitting free men. For my part, with God's help, I shall continue to do what I see as my sacred duty to our motherland until the moment of my death. I ask no less of you, for remember that until one has given all, one has given nothing. *Vive la France! Vive l'Armée Secrète!*" Then, as a bugle call sounded, a flag was raised. The banner, a cross of Lorraine superimposed on the tricolor of France, bore a motto selected by Morel: *Vivre Libre ou Mourir*—Live in Freedom or Die.

Soon after the little ceremony took place, the Germans began making plans to starve out the Glières maquis. On February 11, 1944, Milice and Garde Mobile units encircled the plateau and set up barricades on all the known tracks leading to and from the plateau. By the second week of March, the maquisards were reduced to a thin daily ration of rice, beans and potatoes. German aircraft were making

When a guerrilla force seized the town of Oyonnax to stage a forbidden celebration of Armistice Day in November 1943, cameramen who were members of the maquis conscientiously recorded the whole event. In these pictures of the peaceful two-hour operation, the maquisards are shown (from left) arriving by truck, marching in triumph to the outskirts of the town and laying a wreath at a monument to the World War I dead.

regular reconnaissance flights over the plateau, and every day the leaders of the maquis received reports of a massive build-up of enemy troops around the redoubt. Morel, realizing that time was running out, led a desperate night raid to get supplies from a Vichy depot near the Swiss border. In the course of the raid he was killed. His comrades-in-arms carried his body back up to the plateau and buried it at the foot of a flagpole where he had pledged his life to further the cause of freedom.

The Germans soon became tired of waiting for the siege to force a surrender. They made plans to attack with a division of alpine troops, plus units of the Milice and the Garde Mobile—in all, nearly 12,000 men, supported by heavy artillery and aircraft. Set against this massive force were only 458 maquisards, well dug in to cover approaches to the plateau and to escape the dive bombers that were screaming overhead.

The Miliciens and the Gardes Mobiles were given the dubious honor of making the initial assault on March 20. Despite the huge odds in their favor, they were repulsed. Milice Chief Joseph Darnand hastily adopted a new tactic; he personally drafted a leaflet that was air-dropped in quantity on the plateau. "Your situation is hopeless," the leaflet informed the maquisards. "Those among you who have not committed acts of banditry will not be considered as terrorists but as compatriots misled by lying propaganda. To those the French law will apply with the greatest understanding. Frenchmen, return to lawfulness! Lay down your arms. Return at once to your valleys."

The maquisards stayed on their mountain, disdaining so much as a reply. At dawn on Sunday, March 26, four batteries of 88mm guns and three sections of heavy mortars began bombarding the plateau. Luftwaffe dive bombers joined in the attack. While 500 Miliciens mounted an assault against one side of the plateau to draw the maquis' fire, the skilled German mountain troops began clambering up the most difficult approach. Bitter fighting raged all day. Finally, the maquis leaders realized that they lacked the manpower and

supplies to hold the plateau, and they ordered their men to fight their way out.

Of the 458 men on Glières Plateau, 42 were killed during the battle or in skirmishes during the retreat, and 83 were captured and executed by the Germans. The attackers paid a much higher price; the maquis estimated that more than 700 German troops and 150 Miliciens or Gardes Mobiles were killed. But in the end, the whole area suffered for the maquis' stand. Miliciens rampaged through villages around the plateau, burning the farms of suspected maquis sympathizers and searching for maquisards who had managed to escape. Milice interrogators were thorough: When two maquis prisoners were transferred from Milice hands to the Gestapo for further questioning, they had been beaten so badly that neither could speak or see. Since they were beyond suffering further pain and were therefore useless to the Gestapo, the two were summarily shot.

Tragic as the Glières battle was for the marquis, it had an unexpected and dramatic result. Inspired by the heroism of the maquisards, more than 3,000 recruits formed the 2nd Battalion of the Plateau of Glières. By the time the summer of 1944 was done, they would liberate their department before the Allied armies arrived, taking 3,500 German prisoners in the process.

Even while bodies were still being found on the tangled slopes leading to the Glières Plateau, spring came to Europe. In Norway, Denmark, Holland and Belgium as well as France, spirits soared with the budding of trees and a hint of real warmth in the sun. Hopes were lifted, too, by mounting evidence that the Allied armies would be coming soon.

The Allies did come, landing in Normandy on the 6th of June, 1944. In the weeks preceding and following that momentous event, Resistance activity reached its crescendo throughout the West.

Allied planners welcomed this surge of effort by the underground forces. But they feared any insurrection that might result in the useless slaughter of civilian populations.

Messages were delivered to Resistance forces everywhere warning of the danger. The one received by Milorg, the military arm of the Norwegian underground, was typical: "No Allied military offensive operations are planned for your theater, therefore no steps must be taken to encourage the Resistance Movement as such to overt action"—a euphemism for popular uprising—"since no outside support can be forthcoming."

What the Allied commanders wanted was selective sabotage, and they were promptly obliged by Milorg, especially the unit that became known both to Germans (bitterly) and to Norwegians (proudly) as the Oslo Gang. By the end of June, the Oslo Gang had crippled the Germans' aircraft plant in Korsvold, had destroyed 25 Messerschmitt fighters and 150 aircraft engines awaiting shipment to the Luftwaffe, had attacked and put out of action a factory in Lysaker making sulphuric acid for German explosives, and had effectively disrupted production at the locomotive works in Kragero, the Norse vacuum oil plant in Loenga and a munitions factory in Kongsberg.

But the most daring Resistance efforts outside of France took place in Hitler's "model protectorate"—doughty little Denmark. On the outskirts of Copenhagen at 7 p.m. on June 6—D-Day in France—members of a group that called itself the Middle-Class Partisans attacked the huge Globus factory, which manufactured replacement parts for German heavy weapons and aircraft. In order to protect the plant, the Occupation forces had taken extraordinary precautions: German engineers had installed bunkers in key places, and the perimeters were patrolled around the clock by armed guards, most of whom were Danish Nazis of the tough Frikorps Danmark, which had been seasoned in battle on the Russian front.

The Resistance group planned its assault meticulously. Machine-gun units were assigned to block key intersections in the vicinity of the plant so as to prevent enemy reinforcements from reaching the scene; all traffic was to be stopped "and German soldiers shot without warning." At precisely the assigned time, the attack teams, wearing helmets with the Danish flag painted on the sides, drove up to the Globus gates and burst through, overwhelming the guards before they had a chance to form. The Danes wrecked plant equipment with hand grenades, completing their mission in 15

THE DISTAFF SIDE OF THE RESISTANCE

When Marie-Madeleine Fourcade, the energetic general secretary for a Paris publishing firm, was asked by an underground leader code-named "Navarre" to help coordinate his intelligence network, she protested, "But, Navarre, I'm only a woman!" "That's another good reason," he replied, pointing out that Germans tended to be less suspicious of females.

The truth was that tens of thousands of women—housewives and students, princesses and prostitutes—contributed to the Resistance movement. They helped with the production of underground newspapers, concealed fugitives, delivered messages, worked in escape lines and joined guerrilla units. Many of them died for the cause, and many others came to assume positions of leadership: After Navarre was arrested in 1941, the same female agent who had originally considered a role in the underground so unlikely took over his far-flung intelligence network.

This gun-toting female maquisard fought Germans in southern France.

Marie-Madeleine Fourcade directed the French intelligence network that was known as Alliance. Under her leadership, Alliance placed nearly 3,000 agents in most of the cities and large ports in France. The organization provided the British armed forces with vital information about German defenses in Normandy prior to the D-Day invasion.

Beatrix Terwindt was a Dutch airline stewardess who fled to London and joined British military intelligence. In 1943 she parachuted into Holland to help coordinate a new escape route. But the Germans, who had infiltrated the Dutch underground, were waiting for her when she landed. She spent the rest of the War in prison camps.

Noor Inayat Khan, an Indian princess who grew up in France, became an SOE radio operator in Paris on June 16, 1943. Two weeks later the Germans arrested a large number of Resistance workers there, and for three months she was the most important operator in France. Then she too was arrested, deported to Dachau and executed.

Twenty-year-old Eva Jorgensen Klovstad joined a Norwegian underground force that was headed by her fiancé. When the Germans broke up the force, he escaped to Sweden, and she took over as the leader. Using a man's name, Jakob, she rebuilt her shattered unit and molded it into an effective force that fought on until the liberation.

Edith "Lotte" Bonnesen, a civil servant in the Danish Ministry of Transportation, worked for the underground press, hid air-dropped agents, planned sabotage raids and eventually took over the coding of nearly all radio messages transmitted to London. When the Germans closed in on her in September 1944, she escaped by boat to neutral Sweden.

Pearl Witherington, a bilingual British SOE agent, parachuted into central France in September 1943 to serve with a local maquis and to act as courier for a fellow agent. When he was arrested the following May, she assumed control of half of his territory. Her maquis, which swelled to 3,500 men, killed 1,000 Germans in four months.

minutes without the loss of a man. The German war machine would get no more of the desperately needed parts from Globus for the rest of the War.

But it was in France, where the invasion took place, that the Resistance performed the most valuable service.

In preparation, London had drawn up detailed D-Day plans that called for Resistance fighters throughout the country to paralyze the French railway system, cut the roads, flood the canals, sabotage the power stations and mount attacks on the fuel and arms depots. More than 1,200 targets were listed for destruction: *Plan Vert* covered railway sabotage; *Plan Tortue* dealt with action against bridges and highways; *Plan Bleu,* the disruption of the Wehrmacht's electricity systems; and *Plan Violet,* attacks on communication networks.

To ensure that these and subsequent operations were carried out in line with the Allies' strategy, General de Gaulle established a new organization, Forces Françaises de l'Intérieur (FFI). From its London-based headquarters, the FFI would coordinate the issuance of orders to all the military Resistance formation in France: the Secret Armies of the Conseil National de la Résistance, the maquis and the Communists (who at times would continue to chart their own course). Some 5,000 Allied soldiers and agents parachuted in and were deployed in teams throughout France to arm, train and discipline the underground armies. They were also responsible for seeing that orders were obeyed, and for guarding against premature insurrection.

Instructions for carrying out the invasion plans were contained in 325 "personal messages" to be broadcast by the French-language service of the BBC on the eve of D-Day. Each message, meaningless to the Germans, was the go-ahead for a specific maquis or Resistance group somewhere in France. Through the long months of April and May 1944, the French waited, tuning in their radio sets to the BBC every night, listening for a few words that would change their lives and help decide the fate of their nation.

At last, at 9:15 on the evening of June 5, 1944, when the lead ships of the invasion fleet were almost within sight of the Normandy beaches, a BBC announcer began to read the vital messages, each of them twice over: "The centipede is a mammal . . . The crocodile is thirsty . . . I hope to see you again, darling, twice at the Pont d'Avignon . . . Jacques needs Melpomène . . . You may now shake the tree and gather pears . . . The dice are on the table . . . The tomatoes are ripe and ready for plucking at Perpignan."

For almost an hour, the announcer continued to read his messages in the same slow, imperturbable voice. Long before he had finished, resistants were creeping from their homes, maquisards were leaving their camps in the hills and small groups were gathering, all of them bent on causing some prearranged havoc.

In the critical Normandy area, Yves Gresselin, a Cherbourg grocer, directed teams that dynamited railroad lines between Cherbourg, Saint-Lô and Paris. Albert Augé, the stationmaster at Caen, led men who smashed the steam injectors on locomotives and wrecked water pumps in the railway yards. A 40-man team commanded by André Farine, a café owner near Isigny, cut the vital telephone line from Cherbourg, blacking out much of Normandy's communications. Next day Major General Max Pemsel, chief of staff of the German Seventh Army, complained: "I'm fighting the sort of battle that William the Conqueror must have fought—by ear and sight alone."

Frenchmen awakened on the morning of June 6 to discover the Allies on the beaches of Normandy and their country in chaos, with trees felled across roads, bridges and the lock gates on canals exploded, trains careening off the rails. Of 1,050 railway cuts planned throughout the country by the Resistance, 950 had taken place.

Now it became critically important for the maquis and other Resistance groups to harass the Germans wherever and whenever they could in order to delay the reinforcements that were being sent to join the defenders at the beachheads of Normandy. The maquisards in Brittany responded superbly, backing up heavy Allied air attacks with rail-line sabotage. Trains carrying a number of Wehrmacht units were delayed for days, and by June 13 the German Seventh Army headquarters was so discouraged by these developments that a control office charged with routing reinforcements to Normandy was closed down.

But by far the most significant single contribution to the Allied landings made by the Resistance was the ordeal it brewed up for the 2nd SS Panzer Division. Bearing the proud designation of Das Reich, the division was one of

Germany's most formidable fighting formations, comprising some 20,000 battle-hardened troops with 99 heavy tanks, 75 self-propelled assault guns and 64 medium and light tanks. The timely arrival of Das Reich on the Normandy beachheads could have exacted a terrible price in Allied lives; and the weight of its armor might have tilted the balance during the touch-and-go first days of the invasion. On D-plus-1, Das Reich was ordered to leave Montauban, in Périgord, for Normandy. The march should have been completed in three days; instead, the division was barely able to get started within that span of time.

As the division received its orders to move, maquisards attacked its gasoline dumps and destroyed much of the fuel. Many hours passed before Das Reich scrounged enough fuel to get on the road. Then it ran straight into more trouble. Maquisards seemed to be everywhere. As the division trundled slowly north, it was repeatedly ambushed. Tank commanders standing up in their turrets were favorite targets for snipers who were hidden in the forested slopes at the sides of the road. SOE's cyclonite land mines—the ones that looked like cow droppings—blew the tracks off the leading tanks.

In addition, countless halts were called to inspect humps in the middle of the road, which appeared through a tank's periscope to be buried land mines; they were, in fact, upturned soup dishes. Twenty-eight maquisard snipers, defending clusters of disabled vehicles on narrow roads, held up an entire Das Reich regiment on the outskirts of Souillac, in southeast France, for a total of 40 hours. In an ambush at the village of Bicteroux in the same area, a bridge on the main road was blown up and 26 maquisards engaged a company of Panther tanks. Twenty of the Resistance fighters died during the battle, but they caused a delay of six hours.

When the news of the maquis' attacks on the panzer division reached the small town of Tulle, southeast of Limoges, maquisards there rose up and stormed the German garrison. The mayor proclaimed that Tulle had been liberated, and the people flooded into the streets in order to help set up barricades. Similar scenes were to take place elsewhere across France in the euphoria that followed the Allied landings; all of these "liberations" were premature, but none of them was so disastrous as that at Tulle. Das Reich's tortured trip took it through the town—and the SS soldiers were by then in a murderous temper.

Brigadier General Heinz Lammerding, the commanding general of Das Reich, announced that Tulle would pay in "blood and ashes" for the killing of German troops. Armored vehicles smashed their way into the town on the 9th of June, and SS troopers rounded up some 500 men and women. Lammerding initially directed that they should all be publicly hanged, but 401 were subsequently released. The remaining 99—including men, boys and women—were hanged from the balconies of houses along the main street and their families were forced by the Germans to watch. Lammerding, some of his officers and a German woman secretary observed the executions from the terrace of the Café Tivoli, where they sat smoking cigarettes, drinking, and listening to phonograph records.

The same day, while a Das Reich battalion was moving through the village of Oradour-sur-Vayres, located about 25 miles west of Limoges, a sniper shot and killed a popular company commander. The next morning, an SS detachment bent on obtaining vengeance ringed the nearby village of Oradour-sur-Glane, whose only crime was that it had a similar name. All of the members of the community were herded into the village square, where an SS officer announced that there would be an identity check. The women and children were instructed to go into the church; its doors were locked behind them. The men were split into half a dozen groups and led to different buildings in the village; there they were shot. The church was set on fire. Of the 653 people in Oradour-sur-Glane, 642 died—245 women, 207 children and 190 men.

Das Reich continued on its grim way, hectored, harried and exhausted. While it was being slowed by the underground, it was repeatedly attacked from the air. It finally

This little French boy was one of 11 survivors of the brutal massacre of 642 villagers at Oradour-sur-Glane by the SS in June 1944. Five survivors escaped by slipping into the surrounding woods while the Germans were rounding up the villagers. Six others, who had been locked inside burning buildings, escaped through holes or windows, eluded the SS soldiers and hid in gardens or in fields until the killers had gone away.

hobbled into Normandy on D-plus-17. The division had suffered heavy casualties and was too late to play any part in the battle for the beachhead.

The forces of the FFI, which had numbered.about 50,000 in January 1944, had swelled to well over 200,000 by July. Frenchmen who had been reluctant to take part in the Resistance when the Germans were still in firm control of the country flocked to enlist in the FFI when it became apparent that the enemy's grip was being loosened. They took the battle to virtually every department in France.

Nameless Frenchmen fought scores of small, gallant actions. In Lisière-des-Bois, southeast of Paris, 320 maquis were trapped in the woods by 3,000 German troops; the guerrillas held off the assault for eight hours—at which point the Germans decided that this tough little nut was hardly worth cracking. They withdrew, leaving behind them 252 dead, against maquis losses of only 27.

Near Vichy, some 200 maquis decided to liberate the little commune of Saint-Amand. They seized the town hall, attacked Milice headquarters and kidnapped the wife of Milice Chief Darnand's secretary. In response, the Germans attacked Saint-Amand by air, then with troops from Orleans in full battle regalia, their faces blacked and their helmets festooned with foliage. The maquis faded into the forests, taking their female prisoner with them; in return, the Germans executed 10 Saint-Amand youths and held 54 villagers as hostages. After prolonged negotiations, an exchange was arranged—54 Frenchmen for the secretary's wife. By then the Saint-Amand affair had kept nearly 4,000 German troops tied up for two weeks.

The plateau of Mont Mouchet in south-central France, where 3,000 maquisards had concentrated by June 10, became another Resistance battlefield. In fighting off the first German attempts to dislodge them, the resistants not only inflicted heavy casualties, but captured two cannon and an armored car. On June 11, some 10,000 German troops, supported by tanks and field artillery, attacked again. By the end of a pitched battle that lasted all day, 1,400 Germans had been killed and 2,000 wounded, according to maquisard estimates—compared with their own losses of only 160 dead and 200 wounded. German reinforcements were brought up, and a week later 20,000 men, with heavy artil-

lery and air support, drove against the Mont Mouchet redoubt. They struck at thin air: The maquis, in the best tradition of guerrilla fighting, had dispersed.

One of the local maquis leaders was Nancy Wake, a beautiful young Australian woman who, while touring Europe in 1939, had met and married a French millionaire. When France fell, she immediately joined up with resistants under her maiden name and worked as a courier for an escape line. In 1943, with the Gestapo on her trail, she was forced to flee to Spain and then made her way to England, where she was trained by SOE as an agent to help instruct the maquis in south-central France. On March 1, 1944, she parachuted back into France, wearing high heels and silk stockings, and carrying a million francs of SOE cash to finance local operations.

Her reception at Mont Mouchet was an ominous one. In preliminary discussions, the maquisards seemed surly, ill-tempered and uncooperative. Later, she eavesdropped outside a meeting from which she had been excluded. To her amazement, she heard the guerrillas agree that one of them should seduce her, then kill her while she was sleeping and steal her money.

That day, one of the maquisards approached her and began to proclaim his passion. She cut him short. "I presume," she said boldly, "you would like to sleep with me." The maquisard, all smiles, declared that he would be enchanted. "That's very gallant of you," she said, "but you see I have no desire to be murdered in my sleep and then to have all of my money stolen." After furiously protesting that he was innocent of her charges the maquisard suddenly owned up. "You win!" he said.

That night, instead of being seduced and murdered, Nancy Wake accompanied a raiding party of maquis into the nearby town of Saint-Flour, where they commandeered tents, blankets and boots from a sports shop owned by a French collaborator. Her fearlessness soon won the respect of the maquisards, and the young woman became the *chef du parachutage,* organizing the supply of arms and equipment from London for maquis groups totaling more than 7,000 men in central France.

When the Germans attacked the Mont Mouchet maquis in strength on June 20, Nancy Wake led a bazooka attack that destroyed an enemy machine-gun post. While driving a van that was loaded with ammunition and mortar bombs, she was strafed by two Luftwaffe fighter planes and managed to jump clear only seconds before the van was hit and exploded. After the retreat from Mont Mouchet, she took part in a bold attack on the Gestapo headquarters at nearby Montluçon. At 12:25 in the afternoon, 14 maquisards in four cars drove straight into the town, screeched to a halt outside the Gestapo building and covered the young woman as she raced up the stairs, threw open a door and rolled a hand grenade into the room. Thirty-eight Gestapo men were killed in the raid.

At about the same time that Nancy Wake and her companions were waging their war in the Mont Mouchet area, other maquisards were fighting perhaps the most vicious of all Resistance battles. It closely resembled the struggle on the Glières Plateau, but it was much greater in scale and lasted six dreadful weeks before it ended in defeat and atrocity. Yet in its own way, the battle was glorious, and it had its own rich, although unexpected, reward.

The scene was the Vercors—still another plateau, some 30 miles by 12, southwest of Grenoble in the Alpine Isère region. On this lofty tableland, which was covered in part by one of the largest forests in Western Europe and which was still inhabited by bears, about 4,000 maquisards had gathered in June to proclaim the Free Republic of the Vercors. Tricolors flew, patriotic speeches were duly delivered, and the leaders of the maquis confidently awaited the arrival of an Allied airborne division—or perhaps even of Charles de Gaulle himself.

Such great expectations were not entirely self-generated.

In a complex series of misunderstood communications with the Gaullist headquarters in London and Algiers, the Vercors maquisards had been led to believe that they would be given the support of an airborne division, and in order to be ready to receive it they had hacked an airstrip out of the mountain wilderness. What they got instead was a large force of angry airborne Germans.

The first German attack came by land on June 13. Days of fighting followed. The maquisards held on, all the while clamoring for help; "Dispatch of men, arms, fuel, tobacco extremely urgent," they radioed. Instead, at the end of June, the Office of Strategic Services—the American equivalent of SOE—dropped a 15-man team into the Vercors with instructions to persuade the maquis leaders to avoid battle and to "incline them toward more useful guerrilla tactics." Two SOE agents were also parachuted in, and they had orders to give similar counsel.

Finally, on July 14, Bastille Day, the Vercors received its first big arms drop: some 80 American bombers unloaded 1,000 containers packed with small arms, ammunition and badly needed clothing—but none of the heavy weapons for which the maquisards had been pleading.

Nearly 20,000 German troops closed in on the plateau on July 18, with columns advancing slowly at eight different places. Despite repeated attacks by Luftwaffe dive bombers, the maquisards held the clifftops for nearly 48 hours. At 9:30 a.m. on July 21, the Germans appeared where the maquis were least expecting them. Under the cover of a heavy air bombardment, 20 gliders slipped silently out of the sky to land on the airstrip that had originally been prepared to receive the Allied airborne division. More than

Shortly after liberation, radios confiscated by the Germans are reclaimed by the inhabitants of Villers-sur-Mer, a village on the Normandy coast freed by British troops during their drive to the Seine River in August of 1944.

200 elite SS troops leaped out of the gliders to attack the maquisards from the rear. At the same time, a two-pronged infantry assault, backed up by artillery, was launched north and south of the plateau.

Neither courage nor small arms were now sufficient to save the Vercors maquis. During the night of July 22, the commander of the Vercors force, who had formerly been a colonel in the French Army, radioed a final and infuriated message to Algiers and London: "Morale of our people excellent but they will turn against you if you do not take action immediately. Those in London and Algiers understand nothing about the situation in which we find ourselves, and are considered as criminals and cowards. Yes, repeat, criminals and cowards."

On the afternoon of July 23, the commander gave the order to disperse. In the process, the maquisards suffered casualties that brought their death toll to 750. Finally the Germans overran the plateau. "Some of the wounded had taken to the caves," wrote maquisard survivor F. J. Armorin. "The SS were dragging them out by their hair, their legs. A dozen or so were loaded on a few hand-barrows, were thrown onto German lorries like sacks, and beaten and stabbed to death. The bodies were driven away and thrown into ditches along the roads. A troop of 16 men who were seriously wounded, covered with blood and supporting themselves on improvised crutches, were marched to a wall and mowed down by machine-gun fire. The Germans beat their faces to pulp with their rifle butts and jackboots. Some 50 men who managed to crawl into a thicket were found by a troop of SS men and beaten to death, one by one."

But the Germans had by no means heard the last of the Vercors maquisards. Despite the slaughter, most of the Resistance fighters escaped and joined other maquis within the department of Isère. Thus strengthened by veterans who had not only endured and survived the fighting on the Vercors Plateau but who thirsted to revenge its savage aftermath, the Isère maquis in southeast France expanded their activities.

On August 10, the German commanders decided to regain control of the entire maquis-infested region. They sent the 157th Infantry Division to launch a full-scale attack to clear mountain passes through the Alps. Small maquis bands fought scores of stinging little actions—they killed 200 Germans and themselves suffered losses of only 21—while the main guerrilla forces escaped into the flickering light of the Isère forests. The 157th Division was still stewing about on

its thankless mission on August 15—when it could have been used to better effect against the Allied invasion of the French Riviera.

The Allied landings along a 45-mile front of the Mediterranean coast were made by three divisions of the American VI Corps under Major General Lucian K. Truscott Jr., a hardbitten veteran of the North African and Italian invasions. Truscott would later pay high tribute to the maquis, who had helped to make the invasion of southern France one of the most successful Allied efforts of the War. "Their knowledge of the country, of enemy dispositions and movements was invaluable," he declared, "and their fighting ability was extraordinary."

The original Allied plan called for the Free French First Army, which had come ashore on D-plus-1 under General Jean de Lattre de Tassigny, to capture Toulon and Marseilles while the American VI Corps, after consolidating its beachheads, wheeled westward to cut off the German Nineteenth Army as it retreated northward up the Rhone Valley. But the maquis swarmed up the parallel Route Napoleon, the historic mountain route from Nice to Grenoble taken by the deposed Emperor in 1815 on his return from Elba. The

maquis staged hit-and-run attacks and supplied the Americans with intelligence, helping Truscott in his armored attack on Grenoble. The capture of the city had been expected by Allied planners around D-plus-90, but Grenoble fell instead on D-plus-7. Then VI Corps units raced northwest toward Lyons, hoping to cut off the Germans streaming up the Rhone Valley. Due to a mix-up during the Americans' headlong dash, much of the Nineteenth Army escaped, but it suffered heavy damage, inflicted partly by maquis.

Lyons had long been a hotbed of the Resistance; many men from the region had belonged to France's only unbeaten army, the Army of the Alps, and had become maquisards after the Germans occupied the south of France in 1942. On August 28, maquis battalions from the Ardèche and the Loire, the Rhône, the Ain and, not least, the Isère with its veterans of the Vercors, were ordered to concentrate west of Lyons. Along with Free French regulars who had already taken Toulon and Marseilles, they were scheduled to attack Lyons from the west bank of the Rhone at 6 a.m. on September 3, while units of the VI Corps struck from the east bank. But on September 2, the German garrison in Lyons abandoned the city and fled northward.

After pursuing the Germans in vain, the maquis settled for

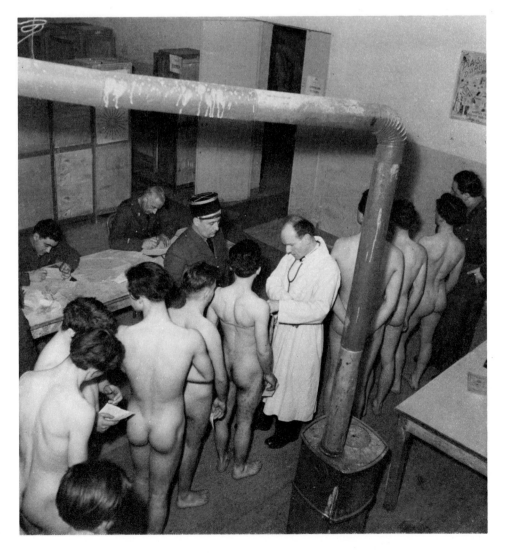

At a belated funeral service in the liberated town of Rennes on September 29, 1944, French officials offer their condolences to the families of 15 Resistance workers who had been tortured to death by the Germans.

Former maquisards, volunteering for the regular French Army, queue up for a physical examination at a recruiting center. In August of 1944, General de Gaulle invited all maquisards to join his army—and more than half of them responded to the call.

half a victory at Lyons. But following the liberation of their city, the Lyonnais took revenge in a scene that was often repeated throughout France and, indeed, all the occupied countries. "People's tribunals" were set up in Lyons and, before cooler heads gained control, they convicted and executed 20 or more collaborators.

Meanwhile, the swift northward advance of the Americans, the French regulars and the maquis was threatening some 80,000 troops of the German First Army with entrapment in southwestern France. U.S. General George S. Patton's Third Army, including French General Jacques Leclerc's 2nd Armored Division, was racing eastward from liberated Paris toward a junction, somewhere near Dijon, with the Allied invasion force from the south.

To escape, the Germans had to get through Dijon before the Allied pincers closed; they were punished everywhere by maquis. In the department of Creuse in south-central France, the Germans were ambushed by a local band of maquisards. "An unending stream of German armoured cars, motor-cars, motorcyclists, lorries and occasional tanks appeared," reported an SOE officer attached to another maquis unit. "The speed of advance was extremely slow—about 5 miles an hour—and there were frequent halts to remove a tree trunk, investigate a supposed trap, or reconnoiter the roadside. All this was sure proof—if we needed one—that the maquis guerrillas were feared, and were succeeding in their main intention of delaying the enemy.

"We had hardly arrived at a nice fold in the ground, bordered by bushes, when the noise of firing broke out on the road some kilometres to the rear of us. The noise of this ambush, though obviously some distance away, caused the whole convoy in front of us to stop. Officers and NCOs dismounted—we could now see every detail plainly—and began scanning the woods and hillsides with their binoculars. Suddenly an intense volume of small arms fire spat out from a spot parallel with our own position, about a hundred yards to the left of us. It was the maquis going into action. There were obviously about six rifles (firing pretty rapidly for untrained soldiers) and two Brens emptying their magazines in rapid, prolonged bursts.

"Then," said the SOE officer, "it seemed as if the whole division went into action against us. Small arms, heavy machine guns, mortars, small pieces of artillery, began plastering the woods on our side of the road over a space of at least 500 yards, and although trees and bushes on our flanks and rear were churned up, nothing dropped near.

"It was so typically German! They found it difficult to locate us, they thought we were more numerous than we were, so they shot at anything moving—even a branch in the wind. They were using a sledge-hammer to crack a walnut—and missed the walnut!"

Blazing wildly away at the pesky maquis as they went, many units of the German First Army made it through the Dijon gap. But lagging behind them were 20,000 men under Brigadier General Botho H. Elster, the tag end of the retreating First Army. Elster's men were pursued and harassed by some 12,000 maquisards of the Corps Francs Pommies, an irregular army distinguished by its uniform of shorts, blue shirts and tricolor brassards. This outfit was named after its commander, Colonel André Pommies, an Army professional who had achieved a singular guerrilla reputation: he had already "suppressed"—i.e., killed—68 Gestapo officers and agents, and he had card files on 3,000 others who were earmarked for similar treatment.

Elster, with many of his men on stolen bicycles, set forth from southwest France on the long march toward Dijon, with Pommies and another 4,000-man maquis snapping at him from all sides. Traveling only at night, Elster got as far as Châteauneuf-sur-Cher, in the very center of France, where he was brought up short by still another maquis. This one consisted of 5,000 men.

Beset by these forces, Elster decided to surrender. But he considered it much too dangerous and undignified to turn himself and his men over to the vengeful, ragtag maquis. Fortunately—or so it seemed to Elster—flank guards of the American army were now in the vicinity. Elster began negotiating with the first ones he found and surrendered to the U.S. 83rd Division on September 8. The leader of the 5,000-man maquis refused to acknowledge the cease-fire: Elster would surrender to him or the maquis would keep firing.

And so, on September 11, 1944, in the town hall of the village of Arçay, a general of the Wehrmacht read aloud to an unsmiling maquis commander the agreement that confirmed the surrender of the last major German force in the south of France.

In the meantime, the Allied advance had reached Belgium, and the Belgian Resistance made a contribution beyond price. The city of Antwerp was critical to Allied plans. "Possession of this port, if usable, would solve our logistic problems for the entire northern half of our front," explained General Dwight D. Eisenhower. The key phrase was "if usable"—and the Germans had vowed to destroy Antwerp before leaving it. Preparing to carry out that pledge, they filled five blockships with about 1,000 tons of explosives and tied the vessels to Antwerp's quays.

The Belgian Resistance, fully aware of what the Germans were up to, took countermeasures. Some 600 men were divided into six assault companies. And on September 3, 1944, as the Allies came within sight of Antwerp, the Resistance struck. On September 4, the Bonaparte and Kattendijk basins fell to Resistance fighters; during the next two days, they took the Royers basin and two bridges on the Albert Canal. Antwerp's great harbor and all its installations were delivered to the Allies intact.

Only 20 miles to the north, the Dutch were eagerly awaiting the arrival of the Allies. On September 17, 1944, Radio Oranje, the voice of the Dutch government-in-exile, announced that the British were nearing the frontier and that liberation was a matter of days. The explosion of Dutch joy was matched only by the panic of the Germans and their puppets, who fled by the thousands in stolen motorcars, on bicycles and even in farmers' carts. But the Dutch celebration proved to be premature. After freeing southern Holland, the Allies ground to a halt at the Scheldt River against a vigorous German defense line.

The stalling of the Allied offensive meant that the remaining occupied countries of Western Europe would not see liberation until spring of the following year. Nonetheless, the Resistance networks of Holland, Denmark and Norway stepped up their activities during the harsh winter of 1944-1945, harassing the Germans with sabotage, with strikes and with demonstrations.

The battle for France ended much sooner. Most of the country was liberated by the end of September, 1944, although isolated pockets of Germans still held out against the FFI. The Resistance forces had turned in a performance that exceeded the most optimistic expectations of the Allied leaders. FFI detachments had provided intelligence that proved to be invaluable to the Allied advance; they had protected the flanks of the Allied armies and guarded the prisoners left behind.

More important still for French morale, the forces of the Resistance had freed much of their country without help from the Allied armies. The Breton maquis, acting independently, had cleared much of Brittany of Germans. The FFI in southern France freed 26 departments—two fifths of the nation. As the towns and villages of France were liberated, Resistance leaders took the reins of government from the hands of Vichy, setting up food distribution centers, town councils and police forces in the chaotic wake of the German retreat. Many of the maquisards, once the fighting in their regions was over, lay down their weapons and resumed civilian life. But many regional maquis units responded intact to de Gaulle's invitation, issued in August, to fight on as part of the regular French armies. By October 1944, some 140,000 maquisards had taken their places in the French Army.

In a salute to the Resistance, General Eisenhower said that the unified forces of the FFI had done the work of 15 regular army divisions, and that with this work they had shortened the War by two months. The price had been high— 150,000 French men and women had lost their lives keeping the flame of resistance burning during the four years that France was occupied.

It would take many more years for the people of France to comprehend fully and to reconcile the terrible ordeal they had endured under the Occupation. But in the summer of 1944, when they exultantly helped to drive the Wehrmacht from their land, they experienced a new hope born of their resistance. It seemed that they had cleared away the deadwood of the past, and that their patriotic solidarity had made a fresh beginning possible.

"Everywhere, Frenchmen looked forward to the resurgence of their country," wrote Colonel Maurice Buckmaster, chief of one of SOE's French sections. "The Resistance was a vital factor in this recovery of the French national spirit. As a triumph of human courage, as a tribute to the eternal hope which leads men to sacrifice everything in the defence of what they believe right, as an indication of the unity which can bind, for however short a time, men of different political, moral and religious views, the Resistance is never likely to be equalled."

SWEET REVENGE

French villagers jeer and curse at a captured German soldier as he is paraded by a resistant through Saint-Mihiel, 140 miles east of Paris, in September 1944.

THE ARITHMETIC OF RETRIBUTION

In the wake of the Allies' Normandy invasion, a French Resistance unit transports medical supplies through a battered village in July of 1944.

Early on August 25, 1944, as French Army units commanded by General Jacques Leclerc entered Paris, Captain Otto Kayser of the German General Staff watched the hectic, joyful scene from a window in the Hôtel Meurice. "Paris," he reportedly said to a colleague, "is going to take vengence for these last four years." Kayser never saw his prediction come true. A few hours later, as he was being marched through the streets as a prisoner of war, a pistol-wielding Parisian burst past the prisoners' French guards and killed Kayser with a single shot in the head.

As Paris went, so went France. Everywhere, ordinary citizens heaped four years of pent-up frustration and hatred on the defeated German Occupation forces, mocking, beating and sometimes killing their erstwhile conquerors. They were even more violent in their attacks on Frenchmen who had done the Germans' dirty work by betraying, torturing or executing members of the Resistance. The worst collaborators were well known; underground newspapers had been blacklisting their names since 1941, and the BBC's French-language service had broadcast nightly warnings that their day of reckoning was approaching. Now, with their German protectors either imprisoned or in flight, many traitors were hunted down and executed without mercy and often without a trial. During the weeks before and after the liberation, at least 11,000 collaborators were summarily executed.

The bloodbath was so widespread that the returning commander of the united Resistance forces, General de Gaulle, hastily established local tribunals to provide legal trials for the accused. After regular courts were established, 767 more citizens were executed, 39,000 received prison sentences and some 40,000 lesser collaborators were punished with "national degradation"—loss of their civil rights. Amid the welter of vindictive verdicts, the courts were surprisingly merciful to the thousands of Frenchmen who had fought for the Germans on the Eastern Front. Former members of the Légion des Volontaires Français and French Waffen-SS were permitted to redeem their honor by volunteering for regular army service in Indochina.

Exhorting Allied troops to shoot all German soldiers on sight, an embittered townsman underscores his point on a blackboard in a village in eastern France.

Under the direction of a French Red Cross official, German prisoners wearing rubber gloves and rubber boots exhume the bodies of Gestapo victims from a cluster of shallow graves in the city of Grenoble.

On the way to a detention camp, despondent German prisoners are forced to appear with their Resistance captors for a trophy photograph. The picture was taken at the village of Maisey-sur-Oise, north of Paris.

THE DEGRADATION OF GERMAN PRISONERS

Amid the hysteria following liberation, Resistance workers were often in the awkward position of guarding captured German soldiers from bloodthirsty civilians, including some whose relatives had been tortured or killed during the Occupation.

Responsible Resistance leaders prevented atrocities but gladly compelled the prisoners to do humiliating or backbreaking labor—sweeping the streets, mucking out barns, digging ditches. In many places, the Germans were forced to exhume the bodies of their French victims from unmarked graves where they had been buried without the rites of the Church.

A maquis leader in southern France ordered 30 German prisoners to recover the corpses of six tortured comrades. When the mutilated bodies were prepared for a proper burial, the captain said to the prisoners: "You may have wondered why we forced you to come here and dig up the men you killed. We brought you here to show you what you have done. And when you go back to your own land, tell your people what you have done so that they will know why the world hates them."

Dragging a frightened collaborator by the hair, a policeman in Rennes heads for the local station. During the Occupation, many of the members of the French police forces had surreptitiously helped the Resistance.

Holding up his hands in self-defense, a kneeling collaborator tries to shield his face from the backhand blow of a resistant in Rennes. His assailants compelled him to shout, "Vive de Gaulle!" and "Vive la France!"

ABUSE AND HUMILIATION FOR COLLABORATORS

All over France, patriots celebrated liberation by rounding up collaborators and settling long-overdue debts of vengeance.

The two pictures on these pages, taken by LIFE photographer Bob Landry in the town of Rennes in Brittany, record the sort of physical punishment meted out to men who had collaborated in even minor ways —such as entertaining German soldiers or soliciting their business. Women who had fraternized with German soldiers suffered more humiliation than pain. Their heads were shaved (pages 200-201), their clothes torn off, and many of them were paraded through the streets draped with signs reading "I whored with the Boches."

Once a crowd had spent its wrath, minor collaborators were usually turned loose— to be scorned and shunned by patriots for the rest of their lives.

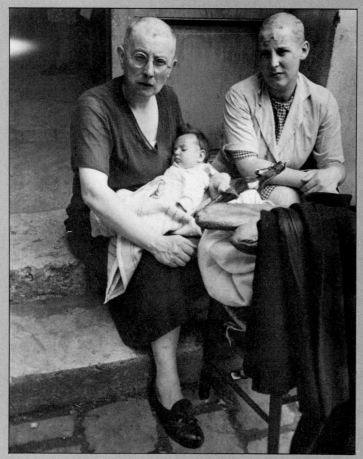

Branded as collaborators by their shorn heads, the French mother (right) and grandmother of a German-sired baby stare out from a stoop in Chartres. Other female fraternizers had swastikas painted on their breasts.

Stripped of his pants and shoes, a man accused of collaboration plods down a Paris street while gun-toting resistants hurl insults at him.

Surrounded by a crowd in a town near Paris, an accused collaborator grimaces and tries to avoid looking at her shaved head in a mirror.

Actor-playwright Sacha Guitry (seated at right), accused of "social collaboration during the German Occupation," is interrogated by members of the Paris Resistance on the night of his arrest in August 1944. He spent two months in prison, then was released for lack of evidence.

Ripped by the volley of a Resistance firing squad, a blindfolded Milicien collapses in death, his body freed by bullets that cut through his ropes and splintered the execution stake. The execution took place in Rennes.

CONTROVERSIAL TRIALS, POPULAR EXECUTIONS

Many of the trials that followed the liberation ended in verdicts that were arbitrary and inconsistent. Prominent propagandists and journalists who had supported the occupiers were singled out for particularly harsh sentences, while little attention was paid to the economic collaborators who had amassed fortunes as contractors and suppliers for the Germans. The inequities of the purge prompted Parisians to make bitter jokes; it was said that a collaborator went free if he had built the Atlantic Wall, but went to jail if he had written that the Wall was a good idea.

There was nothing equivocal, however, about the fate of the cruel, hated troopers of the French Milice—the confederates of the Gestapo and the SS. Members of record were automatically executed—usually by firing squad.

ACKNOWLEDGMENTS

For help given in the preparation of this book the editors wish to express their gratitude to Professor Gustave Abeels, Brussels; Christian Algreen-Petersen, Copenhagen; Joan Bright Astley, O.B.E., London; Vera Atkins, London; Jorgen Barfoed, Copenhagen; Dana Bell, Archives Technician, U.S. Air Force Still Photo Depository, Arlington, Virginia; Jean de Blommaert, Brussels; Margrethe Bohr, Copenhagen; Edith Bonnesen, Copenhagen; Jimmy Bourgeois, Brussels; Colonel E. G. Boxshall, Foreign and Commonwealth Office, London; Father Roger Braun, S.J., Paris; Dr. Richard Breitman, American University, Department of History, Washington, D.C.; Huguette Chalufour, Editions Jules Tallandier, Paris; Diana Condell, Imperial War Museum, London; Pearl Cornioley, Paris; Cécile Coutin, Curator, Musée des Deux Guerres Mondiales, Paris; René Dazy, Paris; V. M. Destefano, Chief of Research Library, U.S. Army Audio-Visual Activity, Pentagon, Arlington, Virginia; Robert Doisneau, Paris; Editions Daniel, Paris; Georges Fèvre, Paris; Kate Fleron, Copenhagen; Jean Gimpel, London; Maître Mireille Gross, Paris; Lady Gubbins, Isle of Harris, Scotland; Gérard Guicheteau, Paris; Robert Haslach, Assistant for Press and Cultural Affairs, The Netherlands Embassy, Washington, D.C.; Knut Haugland, Oslo; Dr. Matthias Haupt, Bundesarchiv, Koblenz, Germany; Claus Helberg, Oslo; Julien Helfgott, Annecy, France; E. C. Hine, Imperial War Museum, London; Edouard Aime Jacobs, Head Curator, Air Museum, Brussels; Professor Louis de Jong, Amsterdam; Soeren Juul, Farum, Denmark; Lieut. Colonel and Mrs. J. M. Langley, Woodbridge, Suffolk, England; Gérard Le Marec, Meudon-la-Forêt, France; William H. Leary, National Archives and Records Service, Audio-Visual Division, Washington, D.C.; Mary Lindell, Paris; Georges Loinger, Paris; London Library, England; Chief Rabbi Bent Melchior, Copenhagen; Meta Melchior, Copenhagen; Henri Michel, President, Comité d'Histoire de la Deuxième Guerre Mondiale, Paris; George Millar, Dorchester, England; Comtesse de Milleville, Paris; Georges Molle, Vieilley, France; The Museum of Denmark's Fight for Freedom, 1940-1945, Copenhagen; Major Flemming B. Muus, D.S.O., Virum, Denmark; Varinka de Wichfield Muus, Virum, Denmark; Airey Neave, London; The Niels Bohr Institute, Copenhagen; Norges Hjemmefrontmuseum, Oslo; Mrs. Cas Oorthuys, Amsterdam; Borge Outze, Copenhagen; J. W. Pavey, Imperial War Museum, London; Yves Perret-Gentil, Comité d'Histoire de la Deuxième Guerre Mondiale, Paris; Janusz Piekalkiewicz, Rösrath-Hoffnungsthal, Germany; Jens Poulsson, Kongsberg, Norway; Group Captain W. S. O. Randle, C.B.E., A.F.C., D.F.M., Royal Air Force Museum, Hendon, England; Marianne Ranson, Comité d'Histoire de la Deuxième Guerre Mondiale, Paris; Michel Rauzier, Comité d'Histoire de la Deuxième Guerre Mondiale, Paris; Harry Rée, O.B.E., D.S.O., London; Roger Schall, Paris; Liepke Scheepstra, Amersfoort, Netherlands; Axel Schulz, Ullstein Bilderdienst, Berlin; Alain de Sedouy, Paris; Frans Selleslagh, Researcher, Second World War Study Centre, Brussels; Lieut. Colonel Terlinden, Brussels; James H. Trimble, National Archives and Records Service, Audio-Visual Division, Washington, D.C.; Gilbert Turck, Paris; Michou Ugeux, Brussels; William Ugeux, Brussels; Dominique Veillon, Comité d'Histoire de la Deuxième Guerre Mondiale, Paris; J. J. van Veldhoven, Voorburg, Netherlands; Hugh Verity, D.S.O., D.F.C., London; Professor van Welkenhuyzen, Director, Centre de Recherches et d'Etudes Historiques de la Seconde Guerre Mondiale, Brussels; Paul L. White, National Archives and Records Service, Audio-Visual Division, Washington, D.C.; Marjorie Willis, Radio Times Hulton Picture Library, London; Marie Yates, U.S. Army Audio-Visual Activity, Pentagon, Washington, D.C.

The index for this book was prepared by Nicholas J. Anthony.

BIBLIOGRAPHY

Aron, Robert:
    France Reborn. Charles Scribner's Sons, 1964.
    The Vichy Regime 1940-44. Beacon Press, 1958.
Beauvoir, Simone de, The Prime of Life. The World Publishing Company, 1962.
Bell, Leslie, Sabotage! T. Werner Laurie Limited, 1957.
Bird, Michael J., The Secret Battalion. Holt, Rinehart and Winston, 1964.
Bleicher, Hugo, Colonel Henri's Story. Edited by Ian Colvin. William Kimber, 1954.
Blumenson, Martin, The Vildé Affair. Houghton Mifflin Company, 1977.
Boolen, J. J., and Dr. J. C. van der Does, Five Years of Occupation. Printed on the secret press of D.A.V.I.D., no date.
Braddon, Russell, The White Mouse. W. W. Norton & Company, Inc., 1956.
Brome, Vincent, The Way Back. W. W. Norton & Company, Inc., 1958.
Buckmaster, Maurice, They Fought Alone. W. W. Norton & Company, Inc., 1958.
Collier, Richard, Ten Thousand Eyes. E. P. Dutton & Co., Inc., 1958.
Collins, Larry, and Dominique Lapierre, Is Paris Burning? Pocket Books, Inc., 1965.
Cookridge, E. H.:
    Inside SOE. Arthur Barker Limited, 1966.
    Set Europe Ablaze. Thomas Y. Crowell Company, 1967.
    They Came from the Sky. Thomas Y. Crowell Company, 1967.
Cowan, Lore, Children of the Resistance. Meredith Press, 1969.
Crozier, Brian, De Gaulle. Charles Scribner's Sons, 1973.
Dank, Milton, The French against the French: Collaboration and Resistance. J. B. Lippincott Company, 1974.
Darling, Donald, Secret Sunday. William Kimber, 1975.
Dawidowicz, Lucy S., The War against the Jews, 1933-1945. Holt, Rinehart and Winston, 1975.
De Gaulle, Charles, The Complete War Memoirs of Charles de Gaulle. Simon and Schuster, 1972.
Delta, Vol. VIII, No. 1. Delta International Publication Foundation, Spring 1965.
Ehrlich, Blake, Resistance France 1940-1945. Little, Brown and Company, 1965.
European Resistance Movements 1939-45. The Macmillan Company, 1964.
Flender, Harold, Rescue in Denmark. Macfadden-Bartell Corporation, 1964.
Foot, M. R. D.:
    Resistance. McGraw-Hill Book Company, 1977.
    Six Faces of Courage. Eyre Methuen Ltd., 1978.
    SOE in France. Her Majesty's Stationery Office, 1966.
Fourcade, Marie-Madeleine, Noah's Ark. E. P. Dutton & Company, Inc., 1974.
Frank, Anne, Anne Frank: The Diary of a Young Girl. Random House, 1952.
Frenay, Henri, The Night Will End. McGraw-Hill Book Company, 1976.
Gallagher, Thomas. Assault in Norway: Sabotaging the Nazi Nuclear Bomb. Harcourt Brace Jovanovich, 1975.
Giskes, H. J., London Calling North Pole. The British Book Centre, Inc., 1953.
Gleeson, James J., They Feared No Evil: The Woman Agents of Britain's Secret Armies 1939-45. Robert Hale & Company, 1976.
Hawes, Stephen, and Ralph White, eds., Resistance in Europe 1939-1945. Allen Lane, Penguin Books Ltd., 1975.
Hilberg, Raul, The Destruction of the European Jews. Harper & Row, 1961.

Howarth, David:
    The Shetland Bus. Thomas Nelson and Sons Ltd., 1951.
    We Die Alone. The Macmillan Company, 1955.
Huggett, Frank E., Modern Belgium. Frederick A. Praeger, 1969.
Hutton, Clayton, Official Secret. Crown Publishers, Inc., 1961.
Jong, L. de, and Joseph W. F. Stoppelman, The Lion Rampant. Querido, 1943.
Kedward, H. R., Resistance in Vichy France. Oxford University Press, 1978.
Knight, Frida, The French Resistance: 1940 to 1944. Lawrence and Wishart, 1975.
Koch, H. W., Hitler Youth: The Duped Generation. Ballantine Books Inc., 1972.
Lampe, David, The Danish Resistance. Ballantine Books, Inc., 1960.
Langley, Lieut. Colonel J. M., Fight Another Day. William Collins Sons & Co. Ltd., 1974.
Latour, Anny, La Resistance Juive en France 1940-44. Stock, 1970.
Littlejohn, David, The Patriotic Traitors. Doubleday & Company, Inc., 1972.
Lorain, Pierre, Armement Clandestin, S.O.E., 1941-1944. 1972.
Luxembourg and the German Invasion, Before and After. Hutchinson & Co. Ltd., no date.
Maass, Walter B., The Netherlands at War: 1940-1945. Abelard-Schuman Limited, 1970.
Macksey, Kenneth, The Partisans of Europe in the Second World War. Stein and Day, 1975.
Mallinson, Vernon, Belgium. Praeger Publishers, Inc., 1970.
Marshall, Bruce, The White Rabbit. Houghton Mifflin Company, 1952.
Martelli, George, The Man Who Saved London: The Story of Michel Hollard. Doubleday & Company, Inc., 1961.
Mechanicus, Philip, Waiting for Death. Calder and Boyars Ltd., 1968.
Michel, Henri, The Shadow War: European Resistance 1939-1945. Harper & Row, 1972.
Millar, George:
    Horned Pigeon. Doubleday & Company, Inc., 1946.
    Maquis. William Heinemann Ltd., 1945.
Neave, Airey, Saturday at M.I.9. Hodder and Stoughton Limited, 1969.
Novick, Peter, The Resistance versus Vichy. Columbia University Press, 1968.
Paxton, Robert O., Vichy France: Old Guard and New Order, 1940-1944. Alfred A. Knopf, 1972.
Petrow, Richard, The Bitter Years: The Invasion and Occupation of Denmark and Norway, April 1940-May 1945. William Morrow & Company, Inc., 1974.
Phillips, C. E. Lucas, Cockleshell Heroes. William Heinemann Ltd., 1956.
Piekalkiewicz, Janusz, Secret Agents, Spies and Saboteurs. William Morrow & Company, Inc., 1973.
Polnay, Peter de, The Germans Came to Paris. Duell, Sloan and Pearce, 1943.
Presser, Dr. J., Ashes in the Wind: The Destruction of Dutch Jewry. Souvenir Press Ltd., 1968.
Reitlinger, Gerald, The Final Solution. A. S. Barnes & Company, Inc., 1953.
Remy [pseud. of Gilbert Renault]:
    Courage and Fear. Arthur Barker Ltd., 1950.
    Portrait of a Spy. Arthur Barker Ltd., 1955.
Riste, Olva, and Berit Nökleby, Norway 1940-45: The Resistance Movement. Johan Grundt Tanum Forlag, 1970.
Ryan, Cornelius, The Longest Day. Popular Library, Fawcett Books, 1959.

Seth, Ronald, *The Undaunted: The Story of Resistance in Western Europe*. Philosophical Library, Inc., 1956.

Shiber, Etta, *Paris—Underground*. Charles Scribner's Sons, 1943.

Smith, R. Harris, *OSS: The Secret History of America's First Central Intelligence Agency*. University of California Press, 1972.

Sweet-Escott, Bickham, *Baker Street Irregular*. Methuen & Co. Ltd., 1965.

Thomas, John Oram, *The Giant-Killers*. Taplinger Publishing Company, Inc., 1976.

Truscott, Lieut. General L. K., Jr., *Command Missions: A Personal Story*. E. P. Dutton and Company, Inc., 1954.

Venner, Dominique, *Les Armes de la Résistance*. Jacques Grancher, ed., 1976.

Vercors [pseud. of Jean Bruller], *The Battle of Silence*. Holt, Rinehart and Winston, 1968.

Verity, Hugh, *We Landed by Moonlight*. Ian Allan Ltd., 1978.

Vigneras, Marcel, *United States Army in World War II, Special Studies: Rearm-ing the French*. Office of the Chief of Military History, Department of the Army, 1957.

Vomécourt, Philippe de, *Who Lived to See the Day: France in Arms, 1940-1945*. Hutchinson & Co. Ltd., 1961.

Walter, Gérard, *Paris under the Occupation*. The Orion Press, Inc., 1960.

Warmbrunn, Werner, *The Dutch under German Occupation 1940-1945*. Stanford University Press, 1963.

Warner, Geoffrey, *Pierre Laval and the Eclipse of France*. The Macmillan Company, 1969.

Werth, Alexander:
    France 1940-1945. Henry Holt and Company, 1956.
    The Twilight of France 1933-1949. Howard Fertig, 1966.

Wright, Gordon, *France in Modern Times: From the Enlightenment to the Present*. Rand McNally College Publishing Company, 1974.

Wynne, Barry, *No Drums . . . No Trumpets*. Arthur Barker Limited, 1961.

INDEX

Printed in U.S.A.